FOOD FOR

Jon Wynne-Tyson has long campaigned for expanding the boundaries of environmental concern to embrace all sentient life. His earlier book, *The Civilized Alternative*, was welcomed by educationalists as a study of society's values and options. His novel *So Say Banana Bird* made a readable vehicle for the holistic argument. His last book, *The Extended Circle*, a dictionary of humane thought, was enthusiastically received and was given the 1985 Animal Rights Writing Award from the International Society for Animal Rights.

Through his publishing firm, which he founded in 1954 after a career which included several years farming, he has made available a number of contributions to humane thought, including Porphyry's *On Abstinence from Animal Food*, Catherine Roberts' *The Scientific Conscience*, Manfred Kyber's *Among Animals*, Esmé Wynne-Tyson's *The Philosophy of Compassion*, *Animals' Rights: a Symposium* (edited Ryder/Paterson), Henry Salt's *Animals' Rights*, Richard Ryder's *Victims of Science*, Clay Lancaster's *The Incredible World's Parliament of Religions* and, on a more domestic level, Janet Walker's *Vegetarian Cookery*.

FOOD FOR A FUTURE

How world hunger could be ended by the twenty-first century

Jon Wynne-Tyson

THORSONS PUBLISHING GROUP

First published by Davis-Poynter Ltd., London, 1975
Revised edition published 1976 by Sphere Books Ltd., London, as an Abacus
paperback
Reissued 1979 with further revisions as a paperback by Centaur Press Ltd.,
and in the USA in hard covers and as a paperback by Universe Books, New
York

Revised and reset 1988

British Library Cataloguing in Publication Data

Wynne-Tyson, Jon, *1924-*
    Food for a future : how world hunger
    could be ended by the twenty-first century.
    1. Vegetarianism
    I. Title
    613.2'62

    ISBN 0-7225-1440-9

Published by Thorsons Publishers Limited, Wellingborough,
Northamptonshire NN8 2RQ, England.

Printed in Great Britain by Richard Clay Limited, Bungay, Suffolk

10 9 8 7 6 5 4 3 2 1

Contents

ABOUT THIS BOOK

Originally sub-titled 'The ecological priority of a humane diet,' *Food for a Future* has been welcomed as offering the first complete argument for vegetarianism and veganism. Its topicality is heightened by mounting speculation concerning the gradual phasing-out of the meat and dairy industries in the face of over-population, depletion of natural resources and a more responsible awareness of our environmental obligations.

Weight					
microgram		μg	ounce		oz
milligram		mg	pound		lb
gram		g			
kilogram		kg	1 g	=	0.035 oz
1 g	=	1,000 mg	1 kg	=	2.20 lb
	=	1,000,000 μg	1 oz	=	28.35 g
1kg	=	1,000 g	1 lb	=	453.6 g
Energy:					
joule		J	kilocalorie		kcal
kilojoule		kJ			
megajoule		MJ	1 kcal	=	4.19 kJ
			1 MJ	=	239 kcal
1 kJ	=	1,000 J			
1 MJ	=	1,000 kJ			
	=	1,000,000 J			
Volume:			fluid ounce		fl oz
millilitre		ml	pint		pt
litre		l	1 fl oz	=	28.4 ml
1 l	=	1,000 ml	1 pt	=	20 fl oz
			1 pt	=	568 ml

Preface

Since the first edition of this book in 1975, public and even governmental attitudes to the food we eat have changed considerably. While human health is at the root of most of the concern, since the early 1970s a growing awareness of our environmental predicament has produced a more holistic outlook, embracing the welfare of non-human sentient life. The realization that a more humane diet is an ecological priority has muted the once common gibe that those who drop animal products from their diet are unrealistic cranks.

The 1960s had shown some stirrings. Fine salvoes came from Ruth Harrison's *Animal Machines* (1964), E. S. Turner's *All Heaven in a Rage* (1964), Catherine Roberts' *The Scientific Conscience* (1967 in the USA, 1974 in England), and John Vyvyan's *In Pity and in Anger* (1969). Brigid Brophy's article 'The Rights of Animals' in *The Sunday Times*, 10 October, 1965, made an impact disproportionate to its length. The fact that these important contributions showed a concern well beyond the confines of vegetarianism indicated that the wind of change held some straws of hope for the most defenceless of humankind's victims.

In 1971, *Animals, Men and Morals* (Gollancz) was published, a collection of essays by a dozen contributors, mostly academics. Perhaps its greatest value lay in its confirmation that the notion of animal suffering was a topic deserving of human attention at university level. But the concept of compassion as part of a more holistic view of our environmental responsibilities still hovered in the wings and, although my own book *The Civilized Alternative* (1972) tried to take that further step for a younger and more general audience, it found hard going until I was asked to expand a section, resulting in the first edition of *Food for a Future*.

Contemporaneously, Gerald Carson's useful if punch-pulling *Men, Beasts and God* had appeared in the USA (1972), and between 1975 and

1980 a significant clutch of books was published on both sides of the Atlantic. The bulk of critical approval was given to Peter Singer's *Animal Liberation* (1976) which, more than any other, put the academic seal of approbation on a re-examination of our obligations towards other forms of sentient life.

Some chronological idea of the books that have marked the change of attitude over the past few decades can be had from the Bibliography on page 186. Not only books, but reports, films, lectures, symposia and media programmes on the welfare and rights of animals produced notable landmarks. The 1965 Report of the Brambell Committee, the 1977 Cambridge symposium hosted by the RSPCA (with its proceedings published in 1979 as *Animals Rights: a Symposium)*, The Animals Film in 1981, Peter Singer's Horizon Lecture in 1983, the International Conference on Religious Perspectives on the Use of Animals in Science in London chaired by Tom Regan (author of *The Struggle for Animal Rights)* in 1984, major reports on the nation's slaughter-houses by the government-appointed Farm Animal Welfare Council in 1984 and 1985, and debates such as that on the motion that 'This House Would Welcome the Universal Adoption of Vegetarianism' in the Cambridge Union in 1987, are examples of the continuing interest in an issue that cannot logically be excluded from the holistic perspective.

Yet, while diet was beginning to be examined in the context of a philosophy for life that met the needs of the day, for most it was the practicalities of change, rather than the ethic, that mattered. Of the many myths surrounding what and how much we should eat, the biggest to be dispelled was that we need animal food at all. Acceptance of this now recognized fact was made easier by mounting scientific evidence that much ill health must be attributed to the refining, processing and chemical manipulation of food and to the long-held belief that we need far more protein than is in fact the case. The use of hormones and other additives in meat production has aroused wide concern for human health, and the virtues of fibre, fresh fruit and vegetables, and the dangers in animal fats and sugar, are now acknowledged by all but the thinnest line of orthodox diehards. Factors such as the savings in fuel from a vegetarian economy and a reduction in atmospheric CO_2, and consequently the 'greenhouse effect', have come strongly to the forefront of scientific thinking. Such attested findings have helped prepare the ground for a more humane diet, if not often for humane reasons.

However, a humanitarian viewpoint has been stimulated by a widespread concern with the world's starving human millions and the realization that so much of this misery could be avoided if land resources were not squandered on crops grown for feeding to animals instead of direct to humans. High on the list of ugly statistics was the Treasury's admission (1988) that, in the near-bankrupt EEC, the subsidy from consumer and tax-payers to dairy farmers for each cow is 'greater than the personal income of half the world's population.'

With huge stockpiles of farming surpluses now an embarrassment even to politicians, there is at last some serious talk and some sign of action about less intensive use of the land and about the alternative uses to which it could be put. As yet no real progress has been made in the use of bio-fuels or towards a silvicultural revolution concerned with planting food-bearing trees instead of producing unwanted crops, industrial estates, golf courses or pheasant cover for the misuse of that excess of leisure by which we are being threatened. But, unless our greatest single material problem – that of human over-population – can be solved by international action, then silviculture must have a role to play as the economics of a meat-and-dairy-industry culture become increasingly untenable.

The phasing out of that industry has already begun. The farming and pharmaceutical interests are reading the writing on the wall and disliking what it says. Despite their active opposition to changing patterns, the trend away from an animal-based diet seems unavoidable, for no sound nutritional, medical or social justification exists for ignoring the fact that pressures on world resources demand more responsible feeding patterns in the indulgent West. At a more philosophical level, what I have termed 'dietethics' is increasingly relevant at a time when enlightened environmentalists and laymen alike are recognizing the indivisibility of violence, and that our treatment of animals cannot conveniently be divorced from our behaviour towards each other.

On every side the practical and expedient reasons for fundamental change are being recognized. At the family budget level, cost alone is a considerable factor in the relinquishment of meat as an inevitable centrepiece at mealtimes. With animal rights now a political issue, the media leave no one in ignorance unless they choose to be. If, as yet, less emphasis is placed on our cruelties to animals than on the benefits to ourselves from abstaining from those cruelties, at least no thinking person, unless with a deeply vested interest, can damn the vegetarian argument as lacking in logic. For that argument is concerned with values, habits and our continued existence.

Of course, any review of a lifestyle may be construed as an 'attack', but this pales in comparison to a meat-eating society's unrelenting abuse of animals, whose consumption is the most ultimate and widespread form of violence our species has chosen to adopt. The animals have for too long been in dire need of some 'spokespersons' and, at last, they are appearing in such numbers and with such unanimity as to pose a real threat to what the poet Wilfrid Scawen Blunt called '. . . the atrocious doctrine that beasts and birds were made solely for man's use and pleasure, and that he has no duties towards them.'

Jon Wynne-Tyson

ACKNOWLEDGEMENTS

Among those for whose help and encouragement I wish to express my gratitude in these necessarily abbreviated acknowledgements are Dr Gordon Latto, Billy R. Boyd, Kathleen Jannaway, Peter Roberts, Geoffrey L. Rudd, Dr Alan Stoddard, the late Michael Storm, Frank Avray Wilson and, of course, the authors and their publishers of those books and journals from which I have quoted or borrowed. In particular I must thank Dr Alan Long for his extensive suggestions for this latest edition.

CHAPTER 1

A vegetable love

*When a sentimental passion of a vegetable fashion
must excite your languid spleen,
An attachment à la Plato for a bashful young potato
or a not too French French bean.*

W. S. Gilbert: *Patience*

Ever since man stopped being 'content with a vegetable love' there has been trouble. Even if you set little store by Adam and Eve, preferring to trace our descent from that equally uncertain era when the drought-induced savanna is suspected of having prompted our ancestors to come down out of the trees and add animal flesh to their natural frugivorous diet, you will have to concede that progress has not always been synonymous with improvement. The trappings and technology of modern civilization have done little to moderate the jungle values we have supposedly left behind us.

To get the personal note out of the way, I have had a lifelong inclination to eat the kind of food that our physiological structure shows we were intended to consume. Resistant from pramhood, as are most children, to meat and cow's milk, it took only the squeals of a pig being dragged to slaughter to set my infant teeth firmly on course for a fleshless future. My mother, being half inclined that way herself, gave into my urge instead of hammering it out of me, as it is out of so many young children who instinctively resist being made to eat substances their bodies were never designed to accept.[1]

But while I believe that the case for vegetarianism can and should be argued on several different levels, there are certain things that worry me about it. The first is the word itself. To many, a vegetable still means a

cabbage, a potato or some other shop-weary accompaniment to whatever slice of animal or bird happens to be the main-course centrepiece.
Growing acquaintance with American, European and Eastern eating
patterns has reduced intolerance towards what so many people, particularly in Britain and America, would once have written off immediately as
a cranky diet, but vegetarians may still be greeted by the 'Ha, ha, ha, how
do you manage to stay standing on a lettuce leaf, ha, ha, ha?' of those for
whom the primacy of meat is as unarguable as the coming dawn.

Yet the definition of a vegetable is clear and covers much. It means a
plant, whether root, stalk, leaf, flower, fruit or seed. More narrowly, a
plant cultivated for food. Almost everything we eat is derived from
vegetables (plants) or from animals. The vast majority of the animals we
eat are themselves vegetarian and are therefore supplying us indirectly,
wastefully and at unnecessary cost with what we can more beneficially
consume at source.

Unfortunately, the word 'vegetarian' still presents to many minds a
quite inaccurate picture of the diet and beliefs of people who exclude
animals (and, in the case of vegans and certain religious sects, all animal
products) from their eating habits. Many, it is true, do become quite
obsessed with what, when and how they eat, and extreme food faddists,
whether vegetarian or not, have often given more moderate categories
an undeserved reputation. This has long been one of the social hazards
of subscribing to unorthodox ideas. Health and food addicts, however,
should not be confused with the ethic, nor necessarily with the practice,
of vegetarianism. In the wide world of food reform there are certainly
many vegetarians to be found, but numerous food reformers are no
nearer to vegetarianism than a Masai tribesman or any other staunch
supporter of the meat-with-or-without-two-veg school.

At this point a further definition is called for. Identifying a vegetarian
as someone who avoids eating flesh of any kind (meat, fowl or fish), the
fourteenth (1973) edition of the *Encyclopaedia Britannica* states that
'most vegetarians use milk and milk products; those in the modern
Occident usually eat eggs also, but most vegetarians in India exclude
them, as did those in the classical Mediterranean lands. Vegetarians
who exclude animal products altogether have taken the name vegans,
and those who use milk and milk products are sometimes called
lacto-vegetarians.' This definition is the one accepted by both British
and American vegetarian societies. The word 'vegetarian' was coined in
1842 from the Latin 'vegetus' (whole, sound, fresh, lively) and should
not be confused with a 'vegetable-arian' (a mythical human whom some

imagine subsisting entirely on vegetables in the limited, colloquial sense of that word – that is, on plant life that for some mysterious reasons excludes even such naturals as nuts, fruit, grains, etc.).

In everyday usage, 'vegetarian' tends to mean someone who cuts meat out of his diet but probably eats eggs and dairy products. 'Lacto-vegetarian' or even 'lacto-ovo-vegetarian' are more exact terms for those who exclude animal flesh but eat everything else, but they are normally used only where precise distinctions are called for. A 'vegan', however, is in a quite definite category. He is concerned to eat only plant life, and in some cases excludes even honey. In this book I have at times used 'vegetarian' where 'lacto-' or 'lacto-ovo-vegetarian' would have been more accurate, and on other occasions have used it generically to include vegans – the context should prevent confusion. But where veganism is mentioned it means only one thing – the exclusion of all animal products.

The second thing that worries me about vegetarianism is far more fundamental and important than any definition, and this is the very fact that it has become an 'ism'. The world is riddled with -isms and -ologies and -anities; with specialists and experts; with divisions, categories and compartmental thinking; and so with barriers, suspicions, ignorance, antagonisms, jealousies, strife, cruelty, wars and a sad array of stupidity and suffering. Although this is not the place to pursue the matter in depth,[2] I believe that if there is one -ism worth hanging on to, it is eclecticism – the method of selecting from various systems such opinions, facts and values as are judged to be sound. Those who resist the restrictions and confusions imposed by 'labels', preferring to seek the elements of truth that are to be found in many systems, and to create therefrom a philosophy that is both subjectively satisfying and points towards a more workable social pattern, are likely to adopt a more natural and compassionate diet simply because this would be a logical step in the formulation of a consistent lifestyle. It 'fits'. This is why I suggest that vegetarianism should not be studied or adopted in isolation, but should be seen as part of a way (a more eclectic and eco-*logical* way) of life that may help our species to attain a higher level of physical, mental and spiritual health than we have known before.

Even leaving aside any importance that may be placed on forming a personal philosophy, there can be no denying that food monopolizes a large part of our lives. Whether we think it a crashing bore deserving as little time and thought as possible or whether we pride ourselves on being gourmets, we all have to spend a lot of time thinking about the stuff; growing, buying, preparing, consuming it; and washing up after it. Anything that affects so deeply our physical and mental environment cannot be left to chance and mere preference. Little that we do affects us more than the nature of the substances we eat and drink – not only in terms of man-hours but especially in relation to our psycho-physical equilibrium. It says in the *Dhammapada*, the most famous scripture of the Buddhist canon, 'All that we are is the result of what we have thought.' It has been said more recently that we are what we eat.

Apart from not taking the role food plays in our lives for granted, economic and ecological facts make it increasingly necessary to consider all the grounds for choosing what and how much we eat. On this score at least there can be little disagreement among dieticians, doctors, food reformers, vegetarians, farmers, demographers, environmentalists, and anyone else concerned with our eating habits and their effect on our lives and surroundings. As will be suggested later, there are other reasons why we should be prepared to question these habits, and I am well aware that much to be said may strike an unresponsive chord in a good many hearts. Nearly all of us dislike breaking with custom, but in the sense of having more facts at our fingertips, we are today potentially better educated than in any other period of history, and this new era of knowledge has brought with it responsibilities we cannot ignore. The problems of over-population, pollution and man's place in the scheme of things compel reassessments in many spheres. Our habits of eating have also to be questioned. Mankind has reached countless crossroads. The one we happen to be at is sign-posted to the need to question practices which might not have called for general scrutiny had not the over-abundance of our species brought home to us that the world is finite; our greed and short-sightedness have already done such damage to our environment, and have so depleted and polluted the earth's resources, that we are in very real danger of self-annihilation.

So this book is concerned not solely with whether soya beans have more protein than beef, with the evidence for one kind of food being better for our health than another, with the moral considerations that should arise from our daily inhumanity to millions of sentient creatures. It addresses all these things and many others, but at the same time it attempts to suggest some kind of synthesis: to show that not only do we owe it to ourselves to examine our eating habits, but also to our environment, to the species with whom we share that environment, and perhaps above all to our children and those future generations whose very existence will be determined by the path we choose to take today. We are beginning to realize that there is a moral order within the rediscovered science of ecology. It is an order that must take account of the future as much as of the present.

I hope that this book will also lead to the discovery that a diet that excludes the meat of animals can be enjoyable, simpler, more healthy and undoubtedly less expensive than orthodox eating patterns. Since the economic pressures in our over-peopled world are anyway going to make the popularization of meat-substitutes inevitable, the sooner we realize that necessity carries positive benefits, the better.

Before going any further I would like to clarify what I mean by two of the words chosen for the original sub-title of this book – 'The ecological priority of a humane diet'.

Most of us think of 'diet' as meaning food that has been prescribed in certain quantities or of a certain kind, but in the past it had a far wider meaning and a much better one. It stood for 'A way of living or thinking'. While its present-day use is perfectly appropriate for this book, I believe the arguments I put forward will be better understood for bearing in mind the broader definition.

'Ecological' deserves even closer examination. Ecology, that 'branch of biology which deals with the natural relations between organisms and their environment' or, if one takes the sociological definition, 'the study of the spatial distribution of a population in reference to material and social causes and effects' (SOED), is more than a useful and topical word. It stands for a concept of life and values in which the practical, the ethical and the philosophical elements are (or should be) given equal weight. Employed in this, its most mature, sense, it goes a long way towards standing for that compound of wonder, knowledge, faith and fierce inner need for a sense of direction and framework of behaviour that first prompted men to believe in God.

As with the word 'diet', the 'ecological' of my sub-title may be used in either the narrow or broader sense. I hope that as the argument of the book is developed the reader may move nearer to accepting the wider interpretation. I believe that our growing concept of ecology is prompting a vision that could be said to be nothing less than a modern yet essentially eternal philosophy for contemporary and future existence. A vision that may destroy *di*vision, perhaps helping to build that much-needed bridge between science and those less material concerns that provide the main evidence that mankind is (or at least can become) more than a race of merely clever apes. It is a vision that, although so badly needed, has been pushed aside rather than never before examined. It was Victor Hugo who wrote:

> It was first of all necessary to civilize man in relation to his fellow men. That task is already well-advanced and makes progress daily. But it is also necessary to civilize man in relation to nature. There, everything remains to be done . . . Philosophy has concerned itself but little with man beyond man, and has examined only superficially, almost with a smile of disdain, man's relationship with things, and with animals, which in his eyes are merely things. But are there not depths here for the thinker? Must one suppose oneself mad because one has the sentiment of universal pity in one's heart? Are there not certain laws of mysterious equity that pertain to the whole sum of things, and that are transgressed by the thoughtless, useless behaviour of man to animals? . . . For myself I believe that pity is a law like justice, and that kindness is a duty like uprightness. That which is weak has the right to the kindness and pity of that which is strong. Animals are weak because they are less intelligent. Let us therefore be kind and compassionate towards them. In the relations of man with the animals, with the flowers, with all the objects of creation, there is a whole great ethic [*toute une grande morale*] scarcely seen as yet, but which will eventually break through into the light and be the corollary and the complement to human ethics.

It is with that 'complement to human ethics', that *grande morale* of which our pattern of eating is so inseparable a part, that this book is concerned.

Notes

1. I ask the precise reader to excuse all such words as 'intended' or 'designed'. No spiritual or anthropomorphic loading is implicit. They are purely convenience terms.
2. I have discussed it more fully in an earlier book, *The Civilized Alternative*.

Chapter 2

The social obligation

Real progress is progress in charity, all other advances being secondary thereto.

Aldous Huxley, *Ends and Means*

If man has gained his intellectual dominance over his fellow creatures by concentrating his evolutionary energies on the development of his brain, it remains to be seen whether he can now maintain his position by contriving a method of living in orderly relations with members of his own species. If he fails to do so, he may yet follow the example of many other groups of animals who have achieved a temporary ascendancy by exaggerated development of some particular structrual mechanism. He may become extinct.

Professor W. E. le Gros Clark, FRS,
History of the Primates

The predatory life . . . brings little progress in social organization . . . Predaceous man unlike other forms of predatory life preys on its own species. With predaceous man civilization itself becomes of predatory type . . . Economic warfare, commercial warfare, class-warfare, are symptomatic of Homo praedatorius. *He exploits cruelty on sub-human lives as well as on human life . . . Man's altruism has to grow. It is not enough for him to stand and deplore. That is less to mend things than to run from them. A positive charity is wanted; negation is not enough. In effect it needs a self-growth, which shall open out a finer self. It requires to absorb in 'feeling' something of the world beyond the self and put it alongside the interests of the very self . . . A great gift – some might say divine – comes to the 'self' when perceiving certain suffering external to itself it so reacts to it that suffering becomes its own, and is shared even as a 'feeling' . . . Altruism as passion . . . nature's noblest product; the greatest contribution made by man to life.*

Sir Charles Sherrington, OM, GBE, FRS, MA, MD,
DSc (Cantab), FRCP, FRCS, *Man on His Nature*

Non-violence leads to the highest ethics, which is the goal of all evolution. Until we stop harming all other living beings, we are still savages.

Thomas A. Edison, *Harper's Magazine*

Although the various 'orthodox' arguments for a vegetarian diet are as relevant as they ever were, the rapid expansion of the industrial societies has created a compelling case for the decline of eating meat. No one reading a newspaper needs to be told of the problems that we have brought upon ourselves by the spread of our species. The 'infestation of humanity', as one writer has put it, means quite simply that it is becoming increasingly irresponsible to eat meat. Even if we do not care about the aesthetics and health dangers or about the needless sufferings of the hundreds of millions of creatures we slaughter every year, we cannot ignore any longer the fact that eating flesh is a wantonly selfish and short-sighted practice.

This aspect will be considered in greater depth later, but think for a moment what the habit of meat-eating involves in terms of the world's food supplies. It means the extensive growing of crops, notably grain, in order to feed them to animals from which, after an expensive interval, we take back in exchange an absurdly disproportionate quantity of food in a form that we hallow, quite incorrectly, as being far superior to the plant-life from which it was derived. In addition to being fed the corn that requires great tracts of the world's land, the animals themselves, even in these days of 'factory-farming', need still further huge areas for pasture.

About four-fifths of the world's agricultural land is used for feeding animals, and only about one-fifth for feeding man directly. This fact, shocking in its implications, has been examined by nutritionists Frank Wokes (editor-in-chief of *Plant Foods for Human Nutrition* and chairman of the Plant Foods Research Trust) and Cyril Vesey (University Department of Clinical Neurology, London) in their paper 'Land, Food and the People', Part One of the series *Perspectives in Nutrition*:

At the beginning of this decade there were about 35 hundred million people in the world ... The rich Western nations occupying about half of the world's agricultural land amounted to only about two-sevenths of the world's population; whereas the poor, mainly Eastern, occupying the other half of the world's agricultural land, amounted to about five-sevenths. Moreover, the poor Eastern people live mainly in the tropics where the yields of crops are often less than a quarter of those in the Western countries. Multiplying the yields factor of about 4 by the population density factor of about 2½, we get a differential of about 10 between the average food crop production of the average Westerner and that of the average Easterner. The average Westerner does not, of course, eat 10 times but only about 1½ times as much food as the average Easterner. But he consumes much more animal food, about five times as much animal protein and animal calories as the average Easterner. He is able to do this only because he has two-and-a-half times as much agricultural land on which to produce his food, and this on the average is several times more fertile. But because the people in Western countries consume much more animal food, he even needs to import food materials to feed his animals as well as himself.

To sum up the world food position: we have two-sevenths of richer people, more spread out, and eating more animal food, in contrast to five-sevenths of poorer people crowded together and eating much less animal food in proportion to plant food.

It should be added that this grossly inequitable situation is being worsened by the advent of factory-farming which is producing a population explosion of animals as providers of human food that is outstripping the human population explosion in a galloping competition for the basic plant foods.

When we consider the work, cost and wastage that go into stock-breeding in order that the world's affluent minority can indulge so unnecessary a luxury, the sheer extravagance and foolishness of it all is staggering. We read in our newspapers about the starving and under-fed millions, and all the time we are feeding to meat-producing animals the very crops that could more than eradicate world food shortage; also, we are importing from starving nations large quantities of grain and other foods that are then fed to our animals instead of to the populations who produce them. The milk 'lakes' and meat 'mountains' have become a grim joke – sad and unnecessary epitaphs to millions of creatures that have been born, bred and slaughtered for the sake of profit.

No one need be surprised by the reference to the affluent *minority's* habit of meat-eating. Were flesh-eating human beings not a minority group, the present world-population would be far smaller than it is (perhaps the only argument that could be made out in favour of eating meat!) With cattle needing many times more land for food and rearing than do people, and returning to us such a small proportion of the food they eat, our planet has already got more than its economic quota of omnivorous humans.

If this extremely uneconomic way of obtaining food had been adopted by all nations, the land resources of the world would long ago have been exhausted. Most of the fertile land devoted to cattle – which eat cereals, root and green crops and various seeds for improved milk production – could show a much quicker and more economical return if used for crops suitable for direct feeding to human beings as 'Food not feed.' Animals eat 20 pounds of protein for every pound they yield as meat. In comparing plant with animal food production in terms of yields per acre in less developed and more developed countries it has been shown that

> the plant protein production from cereals and pulses was three to six times the production of milk protein from the same area under the same conditions. For plant protein from leafy vegetables it was seven to twelve times. When these plant/animal ratios were measured against meat protein they were approximately doubled. On the average about a fifth of the plant protein fed to animals becomes available for human consumption as milk, and about a tenth of it is turned into meat. These approximate fifth and tenth figures which take into consideration the amount of protein needed to rear the animal to the age when it will produce milk, and to maintain it between the different lactation periods, summarized the findings of experts in different countries and in our opinion gave a fair picture of the plant/animal position in terms of protein production. A similar picture was obtained from comparison of the relative consumption of plant protein with that of animal protein in human diets in different countries. In China, India and other countries in the Far East containing about half the world's population, the plant/animal ratios for dietary protein range from six to eight. Only in Western Europe does the average consumption of animal protein become about equal to that of plant protein, and in the USA somewhat exceeds it. (Editorial, *Plant Foods for Human Nutrition*, Vol. 1. No. 2, February 1969, Pergamon Press.)

The conclusion to these findings suggested that plant protein would play an increasingly important part in solving the world food problem, and in the few years since those words were written their prediction has been echoed many times.

It is to our shame that such revelations are far from new. Much further back Sir John Russell, FRS, and others before him, made similar estimates showing incontrovertibly that plant foods, if fed directly to man rather than after processing through animals, can increase the yield per acre by up to ten fold. As an example, soya beans yield seven times as much amino-acid per acre as milk production and eight times as much as egg production. Animals are incapable of yielding more protein and energy per acre than the plants they themselves consume. 'Plant foods (fed directly to man) can result in a much more efficient use of land ... Production of a whole new range of processed plant foods such as texturized vegetable protein (TVP), soya and other vegetable milks and protein from micro-organisms (SCP), is steadily increasing.' (Leader, *Plant Foods for Man*, Vol. 1, No. 1, Autumn 1973, Newman.)

Plant foods create protein from water, carbon dioxide and nitrogen, which is why they are the primary source of protein in the world today, but animals have to eat the plants, or eat other animals, to get their protein. The cow (which needs up to 20 gallons of water a day in full lactation) can convert poor protein and other nitrogenous compounds into protein of a better quality, but it is an extremely inefficient and wasteful machine for so doing. At huge expense it consumes a large amount of plant food and converts it into a small quantity of meat. This above all is why governments, economists, industrialists and international welfare organizations have begun to realize that the sooner the cow, the chicken and other victims of our prodigal way of life are replaced by food made from plant proteins (or even – novel idea – by the plants themselves), the better for the world at large. Mixed vegetable proteins can be as good as, and far better than, meat. When that fact is not only fully realized, but universally acted upon, books like this will be unnecessary.[1]

It is not that we have not known these facts, but rather that we have not wished to face their implications. This would have meant recognizing a moral and economic obligation to sacrifice cherished habits, and the rest of the world can rot before most of us will do that. It is relevant at this point to include the following tables which are based on figures given in *Indian Agriculture in Brief (1966)* (Directorate of Economics and Statistics, Ministry of Food, Agriculture Community Development and Co-operation, Government of India).

It will be seen from the second table that fruits and vegetables need to be taken in greater bulk, but they compare well with other foods as sources of different nutrients if their moisture content is taken into account. Their dry weight is only about a fifth of fresh weight. Leafy vegetables are concentrated sources of calcium, iron and carotene, even on the basis of fresh weight.[2]

These facts and figures comprise only a fraction of the evidence for the vital importance of plant foods in solving the problems of India and other malnourished countries. Compared with milk and meat, plant foods are cheaper sources with 5-10 times the yield of calories, proteins and other essential nutrients. High yields of some nutrients claimed for intensive milk production in the UK are not applicable to those encountered in India. Biological values of staple plant proteins may be made comparable with those of animal proteins by blending different plant proteins and by fortifying them with lysine and with vitamin B_{12}. In India the proportion of the cereal crops that is diverted to animal feeding is less than a tenth of that so diverted in the UK, but much groundnut protein, left in the residue from peanut oil production, is wasted by feeding to animals or even by being used as manure.

As a single instance of the folly of what is going on, each year we take from India, a land with so long an experience of famine, many thousands of tons of oilseed protein to feed battery farm animals. Yet an ounce of protein a day could make all the difference between life and death to a starving child. A thought that presumably does not unduly worry those who insist upon eating meat.[3]

If in having a social conscience we are not merely working through a current fashion that will before long be as obsolete as beehive hair-dos or bustles, what should we be expecting of ourselves in an age when the abundance of information available gives us no excuse for ignorance and inactivity? In the past, the hypocrisy of those who chose limited roles for their indignation and social conscience was largely innocent. They simply did not have the facts necessary to relate cause to effect or to see the total picture.

Today's situation is quite different. We are fed information from all directions. Unlike computers, however, our storage systems are grossly inefficient. The effectiveness of our memory banks is determined not by the total number of facts we take in, but the number we wish to reject. We select our facts dishonestly and as a consequence develop a totally unbalanced 'memory' that makes our actions stupid and our reactions inconsistent, anti-social and ultimately self-destructive. We cannot see the whole because we are so busy trying to preserve and defend the part that suits our personal inclinations and weaknesses.

With around 20,000,000 starving people and many times that number seriously malnourished, on (or off) our consciences today, the richer minority which preserves the unnecessary and wasteful habit of consuming dead animals is having it brought home that the only *eco*-logical next step is to stop eating meat and other animal products. For as we continue to destroy the life-support systems of our planet, the graph of starvation and shortage can only rise, however sheltered from such facts we may be by the media and our own wishful thinking. In our greed to profit from the underdeveloped world, we have already gone to great lengths to popularize meat-eating among nations whose diet was previously largely or wholly meat-excluding. Although in the West meat and milk have been toppled from their pedestals and even 'red' meat is under a cloud, as world income levels have risen, the demand for meat has increased, causing the expanding livestock industries to compete for grain crops as a source of animal feed. Having sold the underprivileged nations the ugly notion that a steak a day is the status goal to aim for, we are now beginning to realize that our campaigns will prove to be self-defeating. We are encouraging other countries to compete for the very resources of which we are already running short ourselves. A-political though the arguments for a meatless diet are and must remain, there can be few more graphic examples than that of the short-sightedness of capitalist economics. But such is the nature of the 'beast', that alongside these efforts to popularize a habit that more than any other needs abandoning, the industrial West is already producing alternatives. Although a fair amount of publicity has been given to this fact in connection with the under-developed nations (see page 20), so powerful are the mechanisms by which the bulk of meat-eaters exclude from their recognition any news which might affect their habits, few read or understood the signs. Yet the manufacture of meat analogues for the Western nations is already a sizeable industry, especially in the USA. In Europe the use of vegetable proteins, whether 'textured' or not, is less taken for granted than in North America, but is already established to a greater extent than the man in the street (or the woman in the supermarket, unless she takes the trouble to read the writing on the packets) realizes. The use of analogues as 'extenders' in meat products is widespread and most people do not even notice.

It is an unfortunate fact of modern life that the right things all too often happen for the wrong reasons. The gradual replacement of meat by vegetable proteins has almost nothing to do with any general concern for the sufferings of animals, nor even with the welfare or aesthetic

Table 1. Relative efficiency of vegetable foods and animal foods as suppliers of nutrients from an acre of land

Foodstuffs	Gross yield per acre (kg)	Approximate amount available per acre*					
		Calories $\times 10^5$	Protein (kg)	Calcium (kg)	Iron (g)	Vitamin A $\times 10^5$	Riboflavin (kg)
Cereals	350	12.0	35	0.10	21.0	3.5	0.35
Pulses	250	8.6	60	0.20	20.0	5.5	0.75
Oilseeds	300	16.5	78	0.15	4.8	1.8	0.90
Milk	360	2.4	12	0.63	0.6	3.0	0.30
Animal foods	20	0.4	4	0.05	0.4	0.1	0.06
Leafy vegetables	5,000-10,000	24-48	200-400	125-250	750-1,500	3,500-7,000	5-10
Root vegetables	5,000-10,000	50-100	100-200	10-20	30-60	50-100	5-10
Other vegetables	2,500-5,000	10-20	50-100	1-2	50-100	75-150	1.5-3.0
Fruits	10,000-20,000	50-100	80-160	3-6	120-140	50-100	2-4
Sugar	2,000	80					

* Calculated from figures for yield and average nutrient composition of different food groups derived from values given in food tables for commonly consumed foods.

Table 2. Different foodstuffs as sources of selected nutrients

Foodstuffs		Approximate amount (g) yielded					
		100 cal	10 g protein	100 mg calcium	3 mg iron	1000 i.u. vitamin A	1 mg riboflavin
Cereals		30	100	330	50	1,000	1,000
Pulses		30	40	125	40	1,000	250
Oilseeds		20	40	200	200	600	330
Milk		125	300	50	1,500	1,000	1,000
Animal foods		70	40	400	150	3,300	330
Egg		60	75	170	150	50	500
Leafy vegetables		200	250	40	20	15	1,000
Starchy root vegetables		100	500	500	500	1,000	5,000
Other vegetables		250	500	250	150	330	1,700
Fruits	(a)	100	1,200	300	250	(c) 100	5,000
	(b)	200				(d) 2,000	

(a) and (b) Fruits low and high in carbohydrate.
(c) and (d) Fruits poor and rich in carotene.

sensitivity of humans. The impulse to explore and develop the market may have come in part from observance of starvation and malnutrition levels, but far and away the greatest spur has been good old-fashioned greed. Quite simply, eating meat is a very expensive habit all along the line. It costs more to produce and more to buy than any other staple part of our diet, so much so that at the time of writing many families are already down to one meat meal a week for the unpraiseworthy but significant reason that they cannot afford more.

With the arrival of meat analogues, however, palatable and nutritious protein is available to anyone at a cost below that of many standard items of our diet – and certainly well below the cost of meat. What is more, as the acceptance and use of analogues increase, they promise to be available at prices comparable to some of the least expensive items on the shopping list – such as beans and peas, for instance – for that is what many of the analogues are made of. The process of converting vege-tables into protein without employing the intermediary of a living animal is, or as demand grows will be, in all essentials extremely simple and inexpensive. Quite a lot of the present cost lies in the research necessary to produce the texture and flavour of dead animals – a concern at which future generations may well look back with amused incredulity, for there can be little doubt that as acceptance of such vegetable proteins as tofu, humous, and other 'ethnic' alternatives increases, more textures and flavours will become available and may in time largely or entirely replace those really very limited meat flavours which today so many of us, through sheer custom, value so highly. However, new food sources, whether of textured or direct plant form, must fit into the accepted dietary patterns of developing countries. Food scientists in Illinois have been concentrating on developing simple ways of preparing whole soya beans, using equipment which can be found in any village. They have found easy ways of preventing the slightly unpleasant flavour of cooked soya beans from developing and have also produced a range of dry flaky foods to which other natural ingredients can be added for flavour. Such flakes and flours can be used to prepare traditional breads, chapatis, tortillas and so forth in conjunction with local cereals. A prototype baby-weaning food and a milky beverage are already proving very successful in India.

In his paper 'More Protein from Field and Factory', W. F. J. Cuth-bertson of Glaxo Research Limited wrote:

> There is in fact now a possibility not only of banishing hunger and malnutrition from the world, but also of reducing much expensive and

disagreeable farm work such as the rearing and slaughter of animals . . . In the production of meat analogues most of the original protein becomes available for human consumption . . . Protein cannot be fully utilized without sufficient calories. In populations existing at the borderline between hunger and starvation, the children often receive protein in quantities which would be adequate if they took enough calories, i.e., total food of all types. Because they do not have that food they manifest signs of protein deficiency. This 'induced' protein-calorie deficiency can often be abolished rapidly if enough extra food can be given to prevent hunger. In such circumstances the protein content of this extra food may be of small consequence. In the development of food crops most emphasis has been placed on the production of cereals – rice, wheat and maize – because these constitute the staple food of many people and supply a large propor-tion of the protein and calories that they require. Indeed, if enough cereal is provided to a population to prevent hunger, then that diet will also supply enough protein for all except the young children . . . The protein in meat analogues can be of high biological value, equivalent to that of meat . . . there is also a bonus benefit, compared with meat, of low cholesterol levels . . . The fact that the basic proteinaceous materials for structured proteins are closely standardized chemically and physically helps the manufacturer to produce food items with uniform characteristics. A further advantage to both manufacturer and user is the fact that in preparing structured foods there is no risk of contamination with bone, cartilage, fur, feathers or excreta; moreover the absence of bone, fat and skin in the final products makes their use simpler and eliminates waste. Because of the useful characteristics of these new protein foods their consumption is increasing rapidly. In 1966 sales were about $1 million in the USA, but by 1969 had passed the $10 million mark. A growth of sales of some hundredfold is expected by 1980. (*World Health*, November 1971)

Welcome though such recognition of plant values may be, we should keep the facts in perspective. As Magnus Pyke has remarked: 'When people hear of artificial meat, they usually think the important thing is that science is helping to feed the world's starving millions. Not so! Knitted steak made out of soya-bean protein, peanuts or haricot beans does not add anything to the food supply. The people who eat the artificial would get as much nourishment or more if they ate the beans or the peanuts in the first place.' (*Sunday Mirror*, 22 October, 1972)

In essence, this is true enough, though the 'knitted steak' dig is rather unscientific. Soya flour can be compared with wheat flour and, just as bread is a textured form of wheat flour, so textured vegetable protein is a similar form of soya flour. The chief role of the analogues, perhaps, is to bring us back to square one – to help the transition from animal to plant food via substances that taste of the one but are derived from the other. Alex Comfort's statement that 'with the Third World short of protein, it is inevitable that beef – which is as wasteful in production as grouse, and comes from pathologically fat-loaded beasts – will have to give place to textured vegetable protein' (*Guardian*, 8 February, 1973) was, indeed, a statement of inevitability rather than necessity. If we refuse to do the sensible thing the sensible way (that is, by the exercise of our reason), then we have to be tempted like small children. The way things are going, what matters most is just how quickly we can be persuaded to fall into temptation.

Yet we must not give too much weight to mere changes in fashion. British farmers' current interest in 'low-tech' methods based on grass for sheep, goats and deer is a local adjustment to the predicament brought by vast surpluses, not proof of any fundamental distrust of an insane system and philosophy.

Linked with what we are beginning to see to be our social obligation to phase out the eating of meat and animal products is our new-found awareness of man's folly in having ignored the ecological facts of life. As we have been learning fast in recent years, all nature is, or strives to be, in a state of balance. That balance is essential for the well-being of all. Sporadic natural cataclysms apart, the physical world achieves and retains a workable balance except when man, whose inquisitive intelligence far outstrips his intellectual wisdom, attempts to fight against or outsmart nature. Then and only then do the real troubles begin.

Man's interference with the natural world has of course extended far beyond his eating habits. No one today needs reminders of the many ways in which men have tampered with the environment, usually for short-term gain at the cost of long-term damage. If we can accept the Buddhist concept of *karma* we might well judge that the mess we have made of our world is the direct outcome of our irresponsible and greed-provoked actions. If the only release from *karma* is to be obtained by knowledge and abstinence, as the Buddhists and most great philosophies have taught, then the remedy is obvious and precisely accords with what in the West we term ecological awareness. We must develop a better sense of responsibility towards our total environment. However reluctant the diehards among us may be to admit it, this better sense cannot any longer exclude from revision the staples of our diet.

Quite clearly the eating of meat is not going to cease overnight and many would argue that our social obligations should not permit too abrupt an alteration of the *status quo*. They need not worry. None of the hysterical paraphernalia that greets sudden change need be provoked by the facts we have to face. No columns of placard-bearing farmers and butchers need be seen winding through Times Square or down Whitehall. The changes that have to come will doubtless continue to be gradual, though perhaps far from imperceptible to this generation. It is nevertheless important that we no longer withhold from ourselves and from those who are younger the philosophy or the ecological ethic that lies behind the necessity. For although the changeover may not be dramatic, the sooner it comes the better for those who have for so long suffered from our addiction to animal protein. Not a day passes but that the world's environment is damaged both obviously and subtly by the demands we make upon it. We are part of that environment, and cannot escape the consequences of our irresponsibility, however much faith we may place in the ingenuity of tomorrow and in those scientists and technologists who attempt to persuade us that anything nature does man can do better.

Notes

1. The relationship between meat and milk production is close and intricate. The problems of the dairy industry are greatly increased not only by production levels that depend on trends in breeding herds, the importing and exporting of live animals and marketing patterns, but by the high cost of feeding stuffs. With dairy farming now supplying over 70 per cent of all calves for the veal and beef trade, the inter-relationship of the two facets of the industry becomes clearer. When the Sunday joint nearly doubled in cost in about one year, milk threatened to follow suit unless farmers could keep down the level of their compound feeding, so reducing the availability of meat and provoking even higher prices. (Over 600 British farms abandoned milk production in July 1975 alone and the national herd was being slaughtered at the rate of 100,000 a year.) Either way, animal products are likely to rise to even dizzier heights while greedy nations insist on getting their protein second-hand through herds of inefficient four-legged machines whose role in the economy no conscientious time-and-motion researcher could possibly defend.

2. For amplification of this argument, which is particularly relevant to deficient diets in undeveloped countries, the reader is referred to the paper 'Horticulture in Relation to Nutritional Requirements' by R. Rajalakshmi and C. V. Ramakrishnan, Department of Biochemistry, MS University, Baroda, India,

and to other papers published in *Plant Foods for Human Nutrition* (Vol. 1, No. 2, February, 1969, Pergamon Press), a journal of great importance in the nutritional field.

3. In a paper discussing leaf and microbial protein sources, and arguing that the rapid expansion of the yield of food supplies of vegetable origin is essential to beating malnutrition, A. N. Kurtha, MSc, has written ('Potential Supplies of Foods of Vegetable Origin'):

Oilseed meals are at present used mainly in cattle feed and fertilizer. If these were upgraded to human foods, large quantities of proteins would become immediately available to combat dietary deficiencies of protein (Parpa, 1968). These oilseed meals are the dry protein-rich residue left after the vegetable oil has been extracted from the plant material such as soya beans, peanut, cotton-seed and sunflower seed. However, oilseed-meal protein is deficient in certain essential amino acids and therefore has to be used in collaboration with, for instance, legumes or synthetic amino acids to confer a balanced amino acid content. Such mixed foods then have a high nutritive value and are considerably cheaper than conventional high protein foods. Oilseed meals have a protein content of 40-50 per cent, but most traditional methods for the preparation of these do not result in products fit for human consumption. However, it is possible today to produce good quality edible protein from soya beans, coconut, sesame, peanuts and sunflower seeds. After soya bean protein, groundnuts are the largest source of oilseed protein in the world. Groundnuts are deficient in methionine and lysine, but if used in conjunction with lysine-rich legumes the quality of the protein is markedly improved. A number of products based on oilseed meals have been developed in Asia, South America and Africa. For example, the Institute of Central America and Panama (INCAP) developed a very popular protein-rich mixture called Mixture 9B. It consists of 38 per cent cotton-seed flour, 29 per cent sorghum, 29 per cent maize, 3 per cent Torula yeast, vitamins and minerals. In India a product called Indian Multipurpose Food Supplement (IMFS) was produced, which consisted of 75 per cent edible grade peanut flour, 21 per cent chick pea flour, vitamins and minerals. This has a protein content of 42 per cent.

Groundnut protein is the most important constituent of Indian famine relief foods. In 1970 Britain imported from India groundnut meal the equivalent of a year's ration for 13,000,000 children, expressly to feed animals. In 1973 some 150,000 tons of oilseed protein were imported. Government spokesmen have suggested that much of it would be destroyed by pests or damp if it were not imported, but a genuine foreign aid programme should include know-how and equipment to enable hungry countries to help themselves.

CHAPTER 3

The aberrant ape

Monkeys are far removed from man, but the chimpanzee is biochemically *extraordinarily close, though even he is behaviourally very far
removed from man. To be precise, man's relationship with chimpanzee
is closer* biochemically *than that of dog with fox or cat with lion . . . It
is not just wild and careless theorizing that leads ethologists nowadays to
spend so much time with the chimpanzee, the gorilla, and the orangutan.*

W. H. Thorpe, *Animal Nature and Human Nature*

*Apes and men were fundamentally vegetarian, just as otters and ferrets
were fundamentally flesh-eaters.*
Sir Peter Chalmers Mitchell, late Secretary of the Zoological
Society of London

*The apes and monkeys, which man nearly resembles in his dentition,
derive their staple food from fruits, grain, the kernels of nuts, and other
forms in which the most sapid and nutritious tissues of the vegetable
kingdom are elaborated; and the close resemblance . . . shows that man
was, from the beginning, adapted to eat the fruit of the trees of the
garden.*

Professor Sir Richard Owen, FRS

*Fruits, roots and the succulent parts of vegetables appear to be the
natural food of man: his hands afford him a facility in gathering them;
and his short and comparatively weak jaws, his short canine teeth not
passing beyond the common line of the others, and the tubercular teeth,*

would not permit him either to feed on herbage or devour flesh, unless those aliments were previously prepared by the culinary processes.

Baron Cuvier

Man by nature was never made to be a carnivorous animal, nor is he armed for prey or rapine, with jagged and pointed teeth, and claws to rend and tear; but with gentle hands to gather fruit and vegetables, and with teeth to chew and eat them.

John Ray, FRS

Not everyone is concerned about his social obligations. Many of us are occupied with extracting from life the maximum gain for the minimum cost. If principle is involved, it is increasingly likely to be the pleasure principle. To the hedonist a social conscience is strictly for the next man down the line. Very well, then that is how things are, but so far from this providing the pleasure-chaser with a reason for ignoring the argument of this book, he more than most needs to focus his attention on one aspect in particular. Although development of a social conscience posits long-term considerations that your 'What's-in-it-for-me?' character may feel he can afford to ignore, there is one short-term need that no thorough-going hedonist can do without, and that is good health.

In every organism good health depends upon observance of certain rules. In recent years this fact has been made increasingly obvious to students of the environment. The science of ecology has prompted a now rapidly spreading awareness of the fact that natural laws cannot be successfully flouted. Something has to give.

One of the most obvious facts that a more broadly based study of the world has made clear is that every animal is adapted to take a special kind of food. Feed a tiger on lettuce and you get a sick tiger. Feed a pony on slices of ham and the knacker will be in business. The right food means life. The wrong food can mean anything from diminished physical and mental activity to disease and even death. If anyone seriously doubts that statement he might as well return this book to its shelf and either take out a hunk of escapist fiction or steep himself in some basic texts. The graveyards are full of wishful thinkers.

The importance of food in our lives is not, of course, confined to the arguments for or against a flesh diet. There is no lack of books on nutrition, a great many of which emphasize our growing realization that the processes by which so-called civilized man 'improves' his food are in need of urgent review. Every day more evidence is produced to strengthen the case against the refining, preserving, dyeing and general tampering that goes on with almost everything we eat.

The case against growth-promoting hormones and antibiotics for livestock cannot seriously be challenged. The meat industry's claim that 'hormone-free meat doesn't exist, as all flesh contains natural hormones', must be seen for the red herring it is. The injection of an unnatural hormone such as stilboestrol is not justified by the existence of endemic hormones. The natural and the exogenous should not be confused.

Habit, vested interest, and the 'British disease' still prompt mutterings of the politically-inspired 'anti-science overtones' to be found in the EEC, and a black market in growth promoters has been forecast now that the European Parliament's ban has been ratified. Reluctantly, farmers have begun to accept the need to reduce nitrogen to limit crops or even to take land out of production in the face of growing 'mountains', but the mood for change is agonizingly slow and only economic disincentives or overwhelming evidence of the harm being done to human health by chemical pollution and bad husbandry are likely to accelerate its pace. In the light of public response to the actions required by such epidemics as lung cancer and AIDS, however, this may be an over-optimistic prediction.

But mere food-centred health-faddism can be something of a yawn. If not careful, it is easy to become so concerned about the purity of our food that the sheer worry of it all may have as bad an effect upon our health as eating the stuff we are trying to avoid. There must be balance in everything.

When one reads physiologists' and nutritionists' evidence of the many diseases that are due to wrong food and of how important for our health the right food is, it may seem difficult to understand why the medical profession has not spoken out more strongly. Some might say it would be naïve to expect doctors to encourage the prevention of those diseases by which they earn their livings, but that would be a cynical judgement. A fairer and nearer explanation is that doctors, no less than anyone else, are creatures of habit, brainwashed by the traditions of their calling (not to mention the drug houses) just as much as by the behavioural patterns we all share.

It must still be said, however, that orthodox medicine deserves only our qualified approval until it is prepared to place far more importance on the connection between what we eat and how we are. It is grossly unscientific, indeed truly 'cranky', to ignore man's physiological structure and then attempt to treat the ills he brings upon himself by remedies often as unnatural and suspect as the practices that have caused the disease in the first place.

Such thinking has produced the obscenity of those laboratories in which enormous numbers of animals are subjected to often painful and sometimes barbaric experiments, set up with, unsurprisingly, small success, to find cures for the ills resulting from those non-instinctual habits men have invented and refuse to give up. If we choose to over-indulge our bodies, to pollute and ravish our environment and to cultivate habits that mere common sense should tell us are inadvisable if not suicidal, it is monstrous that we should add to our crimes against ourselves a list of far less excusable cruelties and abuses towards species innocent of responsibility for our self-induced problems.

This is not a digression. In a society where the general practitioner is usually our only guide to better health, it is vital that we understand just how far to trust orthodox medicine to know what is best for us. Too many doctors still lag way behind the knowledge that is available to them. It is hardly surprising that medical science shows such faith in drug prescriptions when one sees how slow so many practitioners are to admit that prevention is preferable to attempted cure. On the other hand, what a task they are faced with in educating most of us to take a blind bit of notice of any warning that might interfere with what we want to do or eat! We cannot blame doctors disproportionately for our own lazy-mindedness and self-indulgence.

The case against such abuses to our physiology as refined flour and sugar (*Pure, White and Deadly* as John Yudkin called his book), excessive alcohol, smoking and so on, is clear and, in all essentials, proven, but it differs from the case against flesh eating in one important respect. Where refined flour and sugar are concerned, the original ingredient can at least be said to bear some relation to man's physiological requirements. They are plant foods. What the chemists and technologists may do to make them more deceptively palatable or cheaper or prettier or bulkier or longer-lasting or differently textured or more packed with those laboratory-produced vitamins that as likely as not have replaced the real thing which has already been fed to pigs, is alarming. They pervert what the science of nutrition should be all about; but at least the foods they meddle with retain some small element that is natural to man. Not so with flesh foods. Here man is attempting to cheat his body outright. He is playing a dangerous game; almost as dangerous as the lettuce-addicted tiger. But the tiger is committing straight suicide; man's game is nearer to Russian roulette. If he eats nothing but meat (especially Western man's processed, cooked, injected, factory-farmed butcher's meat) he will join the tiger long before his natural life-span is completed, but what in fact he does is to adopt an omnivorous diet in which animal flesh and products figure to a greater or lesser degree.

It would be difficult to predict just how far any one of us can go in eating what comes unnaturally. The blood-drinking Masai will tuck into raw flesh and might be taken by some as proof that man can survive as a meat-eater. Survive, no doubt, he does, but while the Masai appear to suffer less from malaria and some other tropical diseases than their vegetarian neighbours, they are far more prone to some degenerative diseases than are the Kikuyu, though among both tribes arteriosclerosis is for some reason virtually unknown. It is thought that the Masai metabolize their cholesterol differently (see Mann, G. U., Spoerry, A., Gray, M., Jarashow, D.; *American Journal of Epidemiology*, 1972). They also seem to have a higher incidence of intestinal disease and pneumonia. If they ate factory-farmed, Western-style, cooked meat and led sedentary lives in a climate less natural to their species, their health pattern would doubtless be far worse.

The Eskimos have offered an extreme example of man's attempt to live almost entirely on animal food. Plagued by degenerative disease from an early age, the majority showing symptoms of hardening of the arteries far too soon in life, with kidney stones and urinary infections common at all ages, the short-lived 'emergent' Eskimo has proved a poor advertisement for his diet, while the effects of social change from increased contact with white civilization since the Second World War have been disastrous[1]; A. Hoygaard (*Studies on the Nutrition and Pathology of Eskimos*, Oslo 1941) reported atheromatous degeneration early in the men's lives and that they lost most of their energy and fitness for hunting before thirty-five. Had the Eskimo not eaten much of his flesh raw, so ensuring a higher intake of the essential vitamin C, he might by now be totally extinct. At best one can only say that compared with the vegetarian Hunzakut, perhaps the finest physical specimen of a human being one could hope to find, long-lived and outstandingly free of disease, the remaining old-style Eskimo is no encouragement to those who defend the virtues of flesh foods.

These are random examples. Although of value, the reasoning behind

such instances is necessarily empirical. Some people have lived to be
ninety on a diet high in animal fats and flesh. Some have died at forty on
baked beans and cabbage, their cholesterol levels no higher than that of
a hamster. Neither example proves anything very much except that we
vary in our constitutions, resistances, heredity, life patterns and tem-
peraments, and lots of things that have nothing to do with what we eat
can kill us.

But what we do all have in common is our physiological structure.
Like it or not, the scientific evidence is that nature did not 'intend' us to
eat meat, whether raw, cooked or in any other way disguised, and from
this it is a reasonable assumption that a diet excluding meat and its
by-products is likely (providing it is balanced and sensible) to bring us
better health than a feeding pattern more suited to a predator.

As T. H. Huxley's still valid table of comparative anatomy shows, man
is 'by design' neither carnivorous nor omnivorous. He is frugivorous,
eating those natural fruits, nuts, shoots and so forth that we think of as
the normal diet of the great apes. He knows that if he feeds one of those
apes, our nearest relatives, on the wrong food, the result will be a dead or
diseased primate. For some reason – perhaps our wayward early role of
scavenger or opportunist hunter – our species and ours alone has the
arrogance to suppose that it is the sole exception to a fundamental law
governing all living things.

The reluctance many of us show in accepting this failure of our
reasoning processes is linked to one of the many popular misconcep-
tions of our time, namely that vegetarianism is only a minority fad. We
are at all times tempted to believe what we want to believe, and life would
be duller if we did not, but it is an indulgence that has contributed more
than most to human misery, besides the exploitation and suffering of
other species.

Times are changing, however, if all too slowly. Few people nowadays
write off all vegetarians as a bunch of cranks, yet, until quite recently,
there was no recognition, even among many vegetarians themselves,
that a dietary pattern that excluded the exploitation of animals was
perhaps the most important step we could make towards the recovery of
that ecological balance we are beginning to see is vital to the sane and
healthful continuation of the world about us.

Acceptance of this fact can be helped only by the further understanding that, so far from the exclusion of meat from our diet being an odd
departure from normality, the eating of flesh is, as has already been
stressed, a minority habit found predominantly in the affluent West. If

'cranky' is a fitting epithet for those who abstain from the majority's norm, provincial-minded meat-eaters who assume that the world ends at Boston or Ramsgate should think twice about using the word.

It is true, of course, that while all the higher primates are predominantly plant-eaters, some species on rare occasions consume animal foods, but these have always been supplementary to the basic diet. Although insect-eating is common among the lower primates, its importance decreases through the higher strata of the primate chain, becoming increasingly rare in the larger monkeys and apes. To what degree the first primates were insectivores is uncertain; invertebrates may well have figured high on their menus. It cannot be seriously questioned, however, that over the past 80 million years fruit, nuts, tree berries, shoots, bulbs and roots have taken over increasingly and are now the dominant sources of sustenance, supplemented by leaves, bark, pith, seeds, fungi, honey and eggs. The fact that the lower primates in particular still consume a proportion of insects and such small creatures as worms and snails is no indication of a truly omnivorous, much less of a carnivorous diet. Many insects, particularly those that feed on leaves and other vegetable matter, are in their consistency closely akin to plant life. Those primitive human tribes who to this day go into the desert or a delicatessen for locusts or a snack of ants are aligning themselves more closely with their primate cousins than with the tiger or hyena.

Although those who would like to prove that the other primates are as nasty as ourselves will always seize upon evidence that apes have killed and eaten vertebrate prey, such incidents are exceedingly rare in the wild and under natural conditions. Where reports of the killing of lizards, snakes, tree-frogs, rats, small birds and young ungulates have been made, it is usually the old-world monkeys (that is, those primates further from man than the great apes) who have been responsible. As Desmond Morris has remarked, meat-eating in baboons and chimpanzees has been hotly argued about. Examples have been given of baboons eating the liver and melkpens of goats and sheep, and while these incidents loom large for the farmers, 'they nevertheless play only a very small, subsidiary role in the general feeding behaviour of baboons. In certain regions they are absent altogether. The same appears to be true of chimpanzees.'[2] (Desmond Morris, *Men and Apes*, Hutchinson, 1966.)

Chimps studied in thickly forested areas killed nothing but insects and ate no meat, but in broken forest chimps have been seen to kill animals, though the extent to which the meat has been eaten is uncertain. As Morris has said, we must not start running away with the

Comparative anatomy From T. H. Huxley's *Man's Place in Nature*

The Carnivora	The Omnivora	The Herbivora	The Anthropoid Ape	Man
Zonary placenta	Placenta non-deciduate	Placenta non-deciduate	Discoidal placenta	Discoidal placenta
Four-footed	Four-footed	Four-footed	Two hands and two feet	Two hands and two feet
Have claws	Have hoofs	Have hoofs (cloven)	Flat nails	Flat nails
Go on all fours	Go on all fours	Go on all fours	Walks upright	Walks upright
Have tails	Have tails	Have tails	Without tails	Without tails
Eyes look sideways	Eyes look sideways	Eyes look sideways	Eyes look forward	Eyes look forward
Skin without pores	Skin with pores	Skin with pores (save with pachyderms as the elephant)	Millions of pores	Millions of pores
Slightly developed incisor teeth	Very well-developed incisor teeth	Dental formula: $6.0.0.0.6$ $6.1.6.1.6$	Well-developed incisor teeth	Well-developed incisor teeth
Pointed molar teeth	Molar teeth in folds		Blunt molar teeth	Blunt molar teeth
Dental formula: $*5$ to $8\ 6.15$ to 8 5 to $8\ 1.6.15$ to 8	Dental formula: $8.1.2$ to $3.1.8$ $8.1.2$ to $3.1.8$	Well-developed salivary glands, especially in ruminants	Dental formula: $5.1.4.1.5$ $5.1.4.1.5$	Dental formula: $5.1.4.1.5$ $5.1.4.1.5$
Small salivary glands	Well-developed salivary glands		Well-developed salivary glands	Well-developed salivary glands
Acid reaction of saliva and urine	Saliva and urine acid	Saliva and urine acid	Alkaline reaction saliva and urine	Alkaline reaction saliva and urine

The Carnivora	The Omnivora	The Herbivora	The Anthropoid Ape	Man
Rasping tongue Teats on abdomen	Smooth tongue Teats on abdomen	Smooth tongue Teats on abdomen	Smooth tongue Mammary glands on breast	Smooth tongue Mammary glands on breast
Stomach simple and roundish	Stomach simple and roundish, large cul-de-sac	Stomach in 3 compartments (in camel and some ruminants 4)	Stomach with duodenum (as second stomach)	Stomach with duodenum (as second stomach)
Intestinal canal 3 times length of the body	Intestinal canal 10 times length of the body	Length of the intestinal canal varies according to species; is usually 10 times longer than body	Intestinal canal 12 times length of the body	Intestinal canal 12 times length of the body
Colon smooth	Intestinal canal smooth and convoluted	Intestinal canal smooth and convoluted	Colon convoluted	Colon convoluted
Lives on flesh	Lives on flesh, carrion and plants	Lives on grass, herbs and plants	Lives on fruit and nuts	Lives on fruit and nuts

* Figures in the centre represent the number of incisors; on each side are the canines, followed right and left by the molars.

idea that chimpanzees are primitive hunters. They are vegetarians – or, more accurately, frugivores, whose over-inquisitive natures may have led them a short way down paths for which a study of anatomy and biology tells us their bodies have not been evolved. In the apes studied by Jane Goodall, meat-eating incidents were extremely rare and those she studied were unusual and atypical of the species in general, living as they did in un-chimplike surroundings. Unlike man, they have known where to draw the line. *Like* man, the upper primates show a degree of thought and feeling that should shame us out of any excuse to ill-treat non-humans. Although the best thing scientists can do for animals is to leave them alone, their many studies have shown beyond all doubt that other primates have societal bonds whose recognition cannot glibly be written off, as the anthropomorphism of sentimentalists.

In *Science* (December 1986) the social behaviour of monkeys, baboons and other non-human primates was discussed by American scientists at the universities of Pennsylvania and Michigan.

They observed that chimpanzees kiss and make up after a tiff, just as humans do. Rhesus macaques achieve the same end by mutual grooming. Adult male chimpanzees set much store by reconciliations, the females playing a leading role in the peace-making process. Adult females frequently initiate a reconciliation by leading one individual to his opponent.

Among many other examples of behaviour similar to that found in man was the mamadryas baboon which stopped a rock from falling on younger members of his troop.

The scientists' admission that monkeys not only distinguish their offspring from others, but also recognize and respect the association that exists between other group members, offers one of many starting points for a total reappraisal of our obligations to other life forms. However, much has been written on the habits and characteristics of the great apes and this is not the place to give them more than passing attention. But while in the present state of our knowledge it is useless to argue to which anthropoid ape man bears the closest resemblance, or to try to insist upon which of the hominid remains discovered in different parts of the world is the highest in the chain linking the apes and modern man, in studying the physiological and anatomical similarities to man and the patterns of behaviour that are found in each layer of the primate chain, it becomes very difficult indeed to rebut the feeling that man, as the latest expression of the *hominoidea*, was 'destined' (if that is not too loaded a word) to be a total frugivore. His departure from that logical phase in his evolution can only have come about through some natural cataclysm of immense proportions or due to some aberrancy prompted by his insatiable curiosity.

We know well enough how perverted mankind's tastes can be. No great ape, given free choice under natural conditions, can match man in his perverse greed for substances and habits that are provably self-destructive or unnatural. Even in captivity, which is not the condition in which any species should be studied or exploited with hope of arriving at balanced conclusions, the willingness of the *Pongidae* to make omnivorous explorations generally stops short of consuming animal products. Only the most inquisitive, and therefore the most mischievous and potentially dangerous primate of all, has gone so far as not merely to sample the flesh of his fellow creatures but to make an industry and a cult of his deviation. If one has any respect for what few facts it has so far been possible to establish, the most we can say is that *some* of man's ancestors certainly were driven by circumstances to adopt a diet that contained an unknown proportion of flesh-foods.

So what has given rise to this idea that *Homo sapiens* has such an unrelievedly sanguinary background? Little more than that aforesaid realization that because the onset of climatic or some other natural change caused a local shortage or even disappearance of the food natural to the higher primates, a proportion of the human line relied to a greater or lesser extent on the flesh of animals. The proof that this was so goes little beyond the discovery of animal bones in and around human or near-human habitations. From this slender evidence the massive assumption is made that every trace of vertebrate life found on or near to primitive encampments supports the notion of man being a natural omnivore. Bone remains can last for many millennia. Proof of a plant diet is usually short-lived and far less easily detected. This doubtless helps to explain why we have been so over-ready to think of early man as a flesh-eater. We forget that a frugivorous diet simply fails to leave behind such obvious traces. Nor is allowance made for all the other reasons why animal remains might have been found in such situations – the attraction of fire; the killing by apes of other species out of curiosity and mischief rather than for food, and of course for their skins for clothing and other comforts; even a degree of early domestication of other species for purposes other than, or in addition to, their consumption. This is not to suggest that some of our ancestors did not eat other animals. They almost certainly did, though absolute evidence of this cannot be said to have been established. A properly scientific approach should take into account the various possibilities that might modify considerably the picture we have of our omnivorous forerunners. The schoolboy image which so many of us (including, it would seem, some of our most distinguished investigators in this field) cling to even to this day – the image of the cave-man with a club in one hand and the thigh-bone of some luckless animal in the other – is dying extraordinarily hard.

Even an ethnologist who claims that some apes kill will concede that the bulk of primitive peoples who have adopted an omnivorous diet rely upon gathering more than upon hunting. The majority of writers and scientists who have investigated these matters are themselves omnivorous Westerners and they may be predisposed to seek in our ancestry predominant evidence for our flesh-eating origins. I believe it would be fair to suggest that few scientists, no less than laymen, have entirely succeeded in resisting the distorting influence of habit, prejudice and wishful thinking. Indeed, to be fair to all concerned, they have not necessarily been confronted with any obligation to show such resistance. We are all to some extent brainwashed by the ethos of our society and our times. The most distinguished palaeontologist alive was once a high-chair problem who had to be made to eat up his 'nice meat'. Once resigned to the habit, and finding himself in long trousers and with the obligation to earn a living, he went on eating what was put before him just as most of us do. Whether or not early man was a scavenger or a hunter, or both, and to what extent, if at all, he was either and for how long and in what areas and so on and so forth – these are still questions that are batted around in a great void of ignorance, half-fact, prejudice, jealously defended preconceptions and the free-for-all atmosphere of a game for which no rules or limits have yet been agreed.

One significant point that the man-was-a-hunter-and-carnivore-full-stop school has almost painstakingly overlooked is that if that were so it is surely strange that he and his kind are not now to be found in the majority. The bulk of mankind, despite the hard-selling of American and European meat industries, is vegetarian – or near enough.

In any attempt to assess the historical pattern, the reasonable and more easily supported view is that in general man has obeyed the dictates of his provably frugivorous anatomical characteristics, his departures from this norm being the exception rather than the rule.

Among the authorities who have questioned the concept of early man as a brutish predator are Drs Lewis and Towers who, in their reply to Desmond Morris, *Naked Ape or Homo Sapiens?*, wrote:

> This tradition [of belief in early man as having been an aggressive, hostile, belligerent cannibal] is a myth, but many of us believe in it as if it were a universally established truth. Hence the further myth of our social evolution from bestial, savage, prehistoric ancestors who were in a continuous state of warfare. Contrary to this view the evidence indicates that prehistoric man was, on the whole, a more peaceful, co-operative, unwarlike, unaggressive creature than we are and that we of the civilized world have in historical time become more aggressive in many ways.

This vision of man's early nature, and the suggestion I cannot over-stress that the bulk of mankind has survived by holding to a natural rather than a deviant diet, are supported by what happened to such aberrant species as Neanderthal man, who was apparently the sole occupant of Europe in the middle of the Pleistocene period and the most violent and flesh-addicted of the hominid branch lines. What *did* happen to him? He died out. Some palaeontologists have noted this fact with something very like pained surprise. For here, surely, was someone who *should* have survived. He was doing all the right things, all on the right pattern of modern Western man. He was violent, he liked his steaks rare and often, he was convinced that force was what made the world go round, and his brain was frequently larger than our own. He had everything going for him, but bingo! – suddenly there was no Neanderthal man. That he failed to make the grade might suggest to those open-minded observers who have not got so near to the problem as to be infected by orthodox storylines that he was simply unable to adapt to a highly carnivorous diet.

Most of our species is to all intents and purposes vegetarian. If primitive man (successful primitive man, that is) was the flesh-eater so many people choose to believe on so very little evidence, we may ask how it is he has survived in the largest numbers as a consumer of foods nearer to those favoured by great apes than, allegedly, by such short-lived sports as Neanderthal man and *Australopithecus africanus* (the extinct, small-brained primate discovered in 1924 by Professor Dart who claimed that it was a hunting and carnivorous hominid). We might also ask how it is that the higher apes and most of the monkeys are virtually vegetarians, whereas we claim to be omnivorous, when it is undeniable that the physical characteristics of all animals can be closely related to the type of food they consume.

As the biologist and nutritionist Frank Wilson has written: 'If our combination of the tiger, rabbit and pig way of eating is right for us, then we should expect to be different chemically from the monkeys and apes. We should be more like that one exception of the primates, the baboon, one of the lowest, nastiest and most stupid of that family, crawling on all fours, with a dog's face and a posterior that is the big joke of the animal world' (*Food for the Golden Age*, Daniel, 1954).

He made a good point. Most of the glib popular pictures of early man suggest that *Homo erectus* was synonymous with *Homo predatus*. The more upright we became, the suggestion goes, the more we slaughtered other species and ate them. Study of the living higher primates suggests the very opposite.

For some years the son of the late Dr Leakey worked on lines that seemed likely to fit at least some of the theories of Robert Ardrey – who subscribed to the view that that primitive double-act, the supposedly flesh-eating *A. Africanus* and the vegetarian *A. robustus*, hammered it out in the savanna, *africanus* exterminating the less assertive *robustus* by the simple method, no doubt, of dealing with him in much the same way as he treated his next meal, though perhaps not to a cannibalistic conclusion – proving that the allegedly carnivorous *Homo* and *Australopithecus* co-existed, though for how long may never be known. Right up to the present, in a sense, perhaps. More recently archaeologists on a Franco-American expedition made discoveries in the central Afar region of eastern Ethiopia that put man at 4 million years old – almost 1,500,000 years older than those remains discovered on the shores of Lake Rudolf in Kenya. If confirmed as the oldest relics of true man, the notion of Africa as his 'cradle' will have taken a hard knock, though even more recent discoveries near the Olduvai Gorge in Tanzania left the state of play at 'deuce'.

In *The Human Story*, edited by Marie-Louise Makris (Commonwealth Institute, 1985), we read that

> . . . recent studies of their teeth reveal that the *Australopithecines* did not eat meat as a regular part of their diet, and were mainly peaceful vegetarians, rather like chimps or gorillas. The popular image of the murderous ape is now as extinct as the *Australopithecines* themselves.

And so it goes on . . . As for the future, however many discoveries have yet to be made, I believe that a more balanced conception of our origins is on the way and that so far from an omnivorous hominid being the forerunner of *Homo sapiens*, it will be seen that *sapiens'* true origin lies in a fructo-vegetarian being from whom later omnivorous man – from climatic and other pressures – branched off as an aberrant and (as time will show) temporary exception. That is to say, 'Darwin's' common ancestor of man and apes did not produce anything so absurdly improbable as a physiological frugivore that had a natural propensity for the diet of an omnivore. By all means let us accept that the common ancestor existed and that apes went one way while man (in his mental growth) went another, but we do not have to make the assumption from this that man was exclusively a meat-eater. It is more reasonable – more in accordance with the facts we know – to suppose that he did, indeed, branch off from the main stem, but only to make a further division (through *force majeure*, not innate inclination) when climatic or other conditions imposed exceptional pressures. True *Homo sapiens* remains a plant-eater while acknowledging that some of his kin have to get a bad habit out of their systems!

This may be a far more scientific and probable explanation than the view that has been fed to us by the bulk of the Western investigators. Many known facts support it. For instance, while the development of a formal agriculture clearly brought with it the exploitation of both animals and the land, even the early millennia of what we think of as the civilized era of our history indicate a lesser worship of, or dependence on, flesh-eating than we find in the West today. Two small instances. The ordinary ancient Roman was a near-vegetarian whose staple food was wheat. Tacitus refers to soldiers who, 'forced for want of grain and vegetables to subsist altogether on animal food, began to sink under their fatigue', while on more than one occasion Caesar admired the fortitude of those legionaries who put up with a meat ration when corn was not available. Even butter was to the Romans a food for barbarians, suitable only (when rancid) as a hair dressing for Burgundians. Lesser pointers are innumerable. When Tollund man was strangled and thrown into the Danish peat bog on some winter's day 2,000 years ago, his last meal had consisted of barley, linseed and sorrel. If such fragments prove little beyond the dangers in generalization, they are of some value.

So far as the argument of this book is concerned, however, the where and the how and the when of man's appearance is not very important. The facts that *are* known are enough to prove, or at least throw a favourable light upon, the points I am trying to make. It really matters not a hoot which of the evolutionary theories takes your fancy. What does matter is that we should keep in the forefront of our minds that whatever climatic or other chance of nature provoked a proportion of our ancestors to take to the eating of animal flesh (a change-over that may well have eliminated all but the more adaptable) and whenever and wherever it happened, nothing in their physical structure was fitted for such a drastic dietary shift. What so severe an abuse to their bodily chemistry did to the health and longevity of primitive man, we cannot say, though it is quite possible that since meat was probably seldom more than a small proportion of what was eaten and was at least fresh and uncontaminated by modern breeding and processing methods, he adapted with more success than he would have done today. Because we simply do not know the answer to problems such as this, the best we can do is to draw reasonable conclusions from what we do know, and the one and all-important thing about which there is no doubt is our physical link with the higher primates and what the higher primates eat. I have been deliberately repetitive about this because it is one of the linchpins of this book's theme.

In view of what is known of the toxic properties in decomposing flesh, with which man's chemistry is not designed to cope, it seems beyond question that its effect has helped immeasurably to brutalize his nature and turn him into the most cruel species the world has ever known. Other factors do of course contribute to mankind's appalling record, in particular to our herd behaviour during wars and other examples of mass hysteria. Brutal behaviour is not the prerogative of flesh-eaters.

Common sense and observation suggest that it is equally beyond question that much of mankind's behaviour is due, as Lewis and Towers indicated in the passage already quoted, to the growth of civilization. That is, to the tensions and stresses imposed by excessive concentration of our own kind. The study of the behaviour of imprisoned and crowded rats has shown horrifyingly close parallels to human behaviour under urban and other stress conditions. That such factors, combined with man's addiction to bad dietary and other habits, account for most of our problems is at last beginning to dawn on even the most closed-minded.

It is difficult not to feel, looking at the world we have made for ourselves, that modern man may yet follow his Neanderthal ancestor into well-deserved oblivion. If ever there was a case for sticking with the fruit and nuts, man proves it. Whatever comfort and hope may be drawn from philosophy, poetry, music, literature and the other accomplishments by which we choose to distinguish man from the beasts, when we weigh the sum of those refinements against the magnitude of his pitiless and incessant exploitation of other species (and, indeed, his own), the contrast only emphasizes what a very great distance we have yet to go before 'human' can be equated with 'humane'. We would be helped to do so if Western scientists, so many of them still obsessed by their vision of 'real' man as being an aggressive omnivore, could begin to work from the premise that *A. africanus* or *Homo habilis* (or whatever other name may be given to him) was, more than the gentler frugivore, the one to take the branch line to an evolutionary terminus. The way the world is going, it would make a lot more sense.

Man has proved, though, to be unique in persisting in those very departures from his nature that eradicate his instincts – or at least suppress them. Just as, until quite recently, the tobacco smoker invariably got away with writing off the critics of, and sufferers from, his wholly unnatural habit as intolerant cranks, so the flesh-eating human, in a mainly omnivorous society, goes largely unchallenged when he defends his habit by appealing to the shut-mindedness and ignorance of the immediate majority who share his preferences.

Although few people in the Western world have not at least heard the moral justification for a meat-excluding diet, what is perhaps the main scientific argument for reviewing our eating habits is seldom allowed the permanence of print. Perhaps this is because, while 'abstract' arguments about ethics and aesthetics leave room for doubt, any case that is made out on the basis of scientific fact cannot so easily be dodged.

We know beyond any supportable uncertainty that numerous practices are not good for us. Many medical and 'social' drugs, smoking, alcohol, urban living, pollution, agricultural chemicals, noise– these are but some of the aspects of modern life that cause stress and load our battered systems with impurities, poisons and a range of irritations and tensions whose long-term effects must be as uncertain as frequently the short-term consequences are beyond doubt. But when it comes to what we eat, the conspiracy of silence has been almost complete, at least where flesh-eating is concerned. Much has been written concerning the adulteration of meat and the chemical 'improvers' and preservatives with which those with a rapidly decaying product to sell try to increase palatability and shelf- (or freezer-) life, but the basic consideration as to whether we should consume flesh in any form is almost totally ignored. That this neglect is in part due to our indifference to the undoubted sufferings of those millions of creatures that are slaughtered every day for our consumption, is obvious enough. However many of the deadly sins man has decided are irrelevant, it is indeed certain that greed continues, shielding our species from the temptation to examine any arguments that might alter its eating habits. The fact remains, however, that in eating meat we are clinging to a luxury that not only lacks any justification, but proves above all just how profoundly unscientific modern man – for all his technological skills – really is. For who but a true crank could dismiss the following facts of comparative anatomy, ignored by those who want to continue to eat meat?

- After intestinal digestion, flesh foods provide an excellent medium for the development of putrefactive bacteria. Flesh-eating animals (the carnivora and omnivora) have a relatively short and smooth bowel permitting the rapid expulsion of toxic food materials.

  Vegetarian animals (the frugivora and herbivora), on the other hand, employ a quite different set of bacteria. Having relatively long bowels designed for food that gives up its nutrients slowly, what they eat breaks down by a process of fermentation, showing that what is bacteriologically suitable for carnivores is unsuitable for frugivores, irrespective of what degree of success the body may appear to have in making adjustments. It should also be noted that the excretions of vegetarian animals are less unpleasant and more often suitable for composting and for incorporation with soil in the natural organic cycle.

- Flesh-eaters have long teeth and in most cases retractable claws adapted for killing and holding living prey.

  Vegetarian animals' teeth shape is different to that of the carnivores, as is the enamel. The teeth of the primates are designed for biting and chewing and not for tearing flesh, nor even the lengthy chewing of coarse foods as in the grass-grazers and grain-feeders. Flesh-eating teeth are like daggers. Grass-chewing teeth are made for grinding. The teeth of apes, monkeys and men come in between. Man's teeth are perfectly fitted for the eating of nuts, fruits and shoots. The dagger-like canines of some monkeys and apes should not confuse the issue. They are for defence, not dinner. Although the rhinoceros and bull, for instance, can show extreme ferocity, their horns and other defensive equipment should not be confused with the aggressive armoury of the carnivora. The protection of mates, progeny and territory is not the same thing as the predatory attack of one animal on another when the pangs of hunger take control.

- Carnivores' jaws open and shut in an up and down direction and they gulp down their food in large pieces with little or no mastication.

  Most vegetarian animals have jaws allowing the slight lateral motion needed for pulping and salivating their food as a preliminary digestive process. Their saliva contains amylases – digestive enzymes (lacking in the flesh-eaters) for pre-digestion of starches in grains, etc.

- The mammalian carnivora do not sweat through the skin but control their body heat by rapid breathing and extrusion of the tongue. Excess moisture is secreted through the bladder.

  Like horses and human beings, vegetarian animals sweat through the skin.

- Flesh eaters lap water with their tongues.

  Vegetarian animals imbibe liquids by a suction process, not by lapping.

There are other differences. The systems of carnivora, for instance, secrete some ten times as much hydrochloric acid as men and other vegetarian animals, this being necessary to dissolve bones in the digestive tract. Another significant chemical fact is that carnivores' kidneys have the capacity to convert uric acid into allantoin, whereas man and the anthropoid apes do not have this facility. Proteins – whether derived from foods which are eaten or from the normal katabolic processes of cellular physiology – are broken down eventually to uric acid which is relatively insoluble. Excess of uric acid may be precipitated as uric acid or as urate stones. Carnivores produce so much uric acid that the kidneys have to take the process one stage further to the soluble allantoin. It is a reasonable assumption, therefore, that man is not designed chemically for the ingestion of vast quantities of protein.

Animal foods are particularly rich in these proteins. To monkeys and men uric acid is an actual poison. Its consequences include gout, arthritis, rheumatism and fibrositis. It is also highly significant that flesh-eaters consume their prey when it is raw and fresh, whereas most humans need to cook and disguise their meat before finding it palatable, some of them even preferring it in an advanced stage of decomposition. And if these further pointers were not sufficient evidence that the diet of the carnivora is not natural to man, the fact that the pattern of the organs in apes and man is identical is enough in itself to indicate that their diet should be similar.

The psychologists have produced ample evidence that, besides being physiologically and anatomically more like man than the tailed monkeys, the chimpanzee is man-like in its intelligence. The gorilla likewise exhibits strong man-like characteristics, though with differences that do no more than underline the differences that are found in the moods of man.[3]

There are still great blanks in the chain of evidence which links the origin of modern man to an extinct form of anthropoid ape, but such blanks do not affect the deductions we make from the anatomical and biological structure we know as *Homo sapiens*. Indeed, it would not be abusing the rules of inference to suggest that the whole matter of man's natural (or 'intended') diet can be put in the form of an elementary exercise in logic:

- man's physical structure is closely akin to that of the great apes
- the diet of the great apes is frugivorous
- conclusion: man is a frugivore.

'Closely', some may reply triumphantly, 'only closely'. Very well, then, but we know of no creature past or present more similar to man. Even if the true missing link should one day be discovered, study of his physical structure will again only prove his frugivorous origins. The link between two frugivorous animals is itself bound to be frugivorous.

Because, physiologically, our nearest relations are the frugivorous anthropoids, anyone with a statistical bent and wishing to render a useful service to mankind could hardly do better than trace the incidence of disease among a cross-section of Western man and compare it with the conclusions of an equally impartial fact-gathering mission to a genuine jungle. For whatever justification we may have for congratulating ourselves on the improvements to physical health brought about by greater cleanliness and other hard-won common sense, we are in some respects more unscientific than ever before in our attitude to the diseases that have been increased and even created by the burdens of modern life. One of the main burdens is undoubtedly our indiscriminate eating patterns.

Anyone who has had anything to do with animals in their natural state will know how fussy they are about what they eat. Many of them would rather die than accept food to which they are not accustomed. They have an unanswerable instinct to guide them and no critical intelligence to interfere. Man alone, bereft of the protection of his instincts, enjoys the doubtful privilege of being able to sustain life, with varying degrees of success, by the consumption of substances that the majority of animals would reject out of hand.

As the higher apes and most of the monkeys are to all intents and purposes strictly vegetarian, it is scientifically impossible and absurd to suggest that we are in some mysterious way a naturally omnivorous exception. To be so it is necessary for our bodies to be chemically different. They are not. While we have our bodies, we carry with us living proof that we are naturally vegetarians. More exactly, fructo-vegetarians. A great deal of our ill health is proof of the same thing, but we have only fairly recently begun to admit that this is so.

Even though the steak-lover may scorn fruit for being nothing but sweet bags of water, ripe fruits contain much sugar, and few can need reminding that a ripe banana, weight for weight, gives as much energy as a steak. Nuts, the pulses and dried fruits are also rich in calories. Before the days of cheap sugar and refined flour, the peasants of the Mediterranean would work through a long day of back-breaking toil on a handful of dried figs and a couple of slices of rough brown bread; the remote farmers of Greece can still be seen faring fine on a diet no more generous, while the desert Arab still lives for weeks and months on a quantity of dates and grains that would shock the surfeited Europeans. The continual battle for the waistline among civilized people proves that our ideas of the quantities of food necessary for life are false – and dangerously so. Like the monkeys, we too can live on much less, and usually in better health, as the endurance of the Greek farmer and the bedouin shows. Much nearer to home, and in colder climates, wiser and more modest nutritional patterns are being increasingly accepted and are providing ample evidence that fitness and vitality are far more successfully maintained on less and better food. Indeed, if we eat, so far as we are able, what is natural to man, we automatically find ourselves eating far less in sheer bulk. The necessity to go to work on an egg (not to mention bacon, toast, cereals, milk, sugar, butter and marmalade) is a commercially-prompted illusion that even the French and other European nations know to be false. For the Athens taxi-driver, 'go to work on a nut' would make a lot more sense, as anyone who has crunched his way down the pistachio-shell-littered streets of that city would confirm.

It goes without saying that how *much* we eat of foods that are not natural to man is even more important than how much we eat of foods for which our bodies were designed. The poisonous substances which are formed in the intestines of people who eat animal foods are among the most deadly chemicals known, such as skatole, indole, tyramine and phenylethylamine. Although the liver does its best to render them harmless, such poisons are inevitably absorbed into the bloodstream, traces entering the brain and provoking headaches, irritability and other psychoneurotic symptoms, especially when detoxification is compromised by the taking of certain drugs. People living active lives in the open air are less affected than sedentary, civilized populations whose bodies have to cope with their self-generated poisons. When Alexis Carrel said that 'food can get at the soul' he was well aware that the putrefaction brought about by eating animal foods bears much of the responsibility for the incidence of nervousness, neurosis and insanity, let alone the more tangible physical ills which fill our hospitals and television screens with evidence that whatever other benefits modern man may be deriving from our all too widely permissive society, he is most certainly not finding that glowing mental and physical health that could so easily be his birthright.

Yet, although so many of us have become temporary omnivores, there is not a fragment of evidence that man's body has gone one step further from the primates' plan than the other anthropoids and the time must come when mankind as a whole chooses between Eskimo and Hunzakut, as the first chapter of this book attempts to make clear. It was only because our primates' gut was shorter than that of the strict herbivores such as the rabbit and the horse that we were able to survive one of Nature's toughest revolutions, the advent of the Ice Ages. We have fared less badly than would many other non-carnivorous species had they taken to animal foods, but we cannot push our luck indefinitely. If we want to increase our chances of really good health (as distinct from the mere absence of identifiable disease, which is about the best that most of us can hope for), we have got to stick with the rules. The rules are clear. No man is a grave. We are physically constituted to eat and derive the most benefit from food natural to the *hominoidea*. Every attempt to flout this inescapable fact adds to the probability, if not certainty, of our suffering from our folly and greed.

This is not, of course, to say that a vegetarian or any other diet can prevent or cure every human ill. As has been said, there are many other factors working against full health in civilized man. Yet the principal health determinant in our lives – the nature of what we eat – is largely ignored. Admittedly, even with our eyes wide open it is virtually impossible today to lead a wholly natural life. The strictest vegetarian, tilling his own acre and living in a loin-cloth on the side of a mountain in the sub-tropics, will find it difficult, if not impossible to avoid descending at times to the level of civilized man and his manufactured, processed, 'convenience' foods.

All the more reason, therefore, for each one of us to go as far as he possibly can to formulate and insist upon an eating pattern that is as sane and truly civilized as the problems of living in a highly technological society permit. There is no single aspect of that pattern more important than the extent to which we cling to a dietary routine more befitting the tiger or hyena than *Homo sapiens*.

Notes

1. The more 'civilized', urban Eskimo communities, largely created since the early 1950s, when industrialization began to corrupt the peoples of Greenland, provide further sad evidence of man's loss of the instinct for self-preservation by obedience to natural laws. Riddled with alcoholism, gonorrhoea, violent crime and mental illness, with half their children being born illegitimate and suicides reaching epidemic proportions, the flat-dwelling city Eskimos have moved a long way in the wrong direction since the dubious benefits of technology and the bureaucratic mind were introduced when Copenhagen became their seat of government.

2. It should be remembered in passing that the baboons, along with other such farouche characters as the Barbary apes, have done much to make men doubt their own frugivorous origins, but they are considerably lower down in the evolutionary chain than are the true great apes – the gorilla, the orangutan and the chimpanzee. These three genera constitute the family *Pongidae* and are by far the closest of all animals to man. The gibbons, whose food consists of leaves and fruit, make up the quartet of anthropoid apes, but have been given the family name of *Hylobatidae* ('tree-walkers') rather than *Pongidae*. All four, plus man, comprise the superfamily *Hominoidea*, within which man alone forms the family *Hominidae*. If you make the rules . . .

3. If we are going to get down to the basics of these comparisons, not only are the teeth and internal anatomy of the anthropoid apes very similar to those of man, but the placenta and embryonic stages show the same agreement. The menstrual cycle in the chimp and the gorilla has the same phases as in woman, and in the chimps the interval is the same. Gestation in all three of the great apes is nine months and the placenta is essentially of the human type. The old-world monkeys have a secondary placenta which is absent in the anthropoids.

   The great apes' divergences from man, marked though some of them may be, are almost all differences in degree rather than in kind. In general the differences correlate with habit. While the apes have retained the primary arboreal habit, this being much exaggerated in the orangutan, man has become terrestrial. The gorilla, however, has become partly terrestrial, so who knows where *he* may end up? The chimp is intermediate between orangutan and gorilla.

The blood of the great apes has been shown to be essentially identical with that of man, while differing from that of the old-world monkeys, and it is of course well known that anthropoids are prone to many human diseases to which other animals are relatively immune. The great apes and men share a peculiar susceptibility to syphilis and apes are almost as prone to typhoid fever as are men. In captivity, chimps are liable to appendicitis, that modern disease of mankind. The reactions of anthropoids to sedatives, stimulants and poisons are again similar to man's, which is further evidence of their indisputable chemical affinity. Even the brain is in all essentials a smaller version of the human brain, no part or organ of one being absent in the other. The differences lie in the proportions of certain parts.

Taking all lines of evidence into consideration, but in particular the anatomical, biological and embryological, the conclusion that physical man has evolved from a lower form, rather than that he made a sudden appearance as though by some special act of creation, seems inescapable. This surely need not dismay those who seek or suspect some spiritually evolutionary purpose or continuation for man. Origins are too readily confused with destinations in the game of what-it's-all-about. The physical evidence does not mean that those who contend that we are nothing more than brainy naked apes have stated the whole (or what may prove to be the eventual) truth. Only those who are far too big for their primate boots can be proud of mankind's performance to date in the evolutionary stakes. When one observes the rate (not necessarily the quality) of progress that has marked man's exceedingly short appearance on earth and when one considers the millions of years that may lie ahead of us if we refrain from destroying ourselves and our environment before the natural cooling of the sun puts the adaptational talents of all animal species to their final test, is it not obvious that our limited, ignorant, perversely misdirected minds and hearts have so far yet to go that our present progress can be seen as mere millimetres along the road that stretches far into the unimaginable reaches of the universe? As our knowledge widens, the eclectic mind can perceive more, not fewer, reasons for supporting a spiritual hypothesis. The amplification of this assertion lies beyond the brief set for this book.

CHAPTER 4

To the cradle from the grave

When we are born we cry that we are come
To this great stage of fools.

King Lear

Make less thy body hence, and more thy grace;
Leave gormandizing; know the grave doth gape
For thee thrice wider than for other men.

Henry V to Falstaff, *Henry IV*

THAT TO JACK SPRAT
Tigers don't eat lettuce,
  Men weren't meant for meat;
Monkeys, men or tigers –
  We are what we eat.

The bulk of the evidence suggests that man, so far from being the natural omnivore many choose to believe, took different dietetic paths according to the pressures of climatic, geographical or other circumstances beyond his understanding or control; it follows that our unthinking adherence (long after any era of necessity) to a flesh-eating way of life invites examination that is not merely based on practical and self-interested considerations, but also contains a strong ethical impetus. I do not mean by this our moral obligations to the species we slaughter for our food (this is discussed in another chapter), but rather to our own kind. In particular to the children we bring into the world and for whom most of us feel some responsibility to do the best we know.

No suggestion is being made that the majority of concerned parents who compel their children to eat meat have anything but the best intentions. They are merely repeating a pattern that is generally accepted by the society in which they find themselves. Few parents' memories go back as far as their own childhood resistance to the food put before them. Nor, let it be added at once, was meat the only cause of battle. Children are often reluctant to accept cooked vegetables, cow's milk, cheese, rich or strongly flavoured dishes and many of the other foods that are the result of our misguided sophistication. The blandness of chicken, fish and the bread-filled banger can help persuade them to be omnivores, as can the salty tang of bacon, but very few children indeed, readily take to red meat, however well cooked, minced or otherwise disguised.

Well-meaning though parents may be, their inability to put two and two together at this stage of their responsibilities is depressing evidence of habit overcoming instinct. It is a sad comment on our evolutionary progress that mankind can have reached a stage where even a mother, at the point in her relationship to her child where she might be expected to be at the peak of her intuitive love and concern, can be so blinded by the mores of society that the last thing she is capable of realizing is that the food that has created such an aura of stress, persuasion and worry as surrounds so many a family mealtime might be meeting such resistance for no other reason than that her child's whole nature is demanding the food for which its body was designed.

Whatever screams and yells may accompany the domestic routine of our primitive relatives, they are not due to juvenile resistance to the weaning process. The gorilla, the chimpanzee and the orangutan have too much inborn common sense to expect their offspring to graduate from mother's milk to minced and boiled flesh, however craftily disguised by being mixed with cooked shoots and roots. For the higher primates under natural conditions, the weaning process is as straightforward and unquestioned as in any other species except man. The difficulties we face with our own children are entirely the result of our perverse sophistication and, above all, our unthinking determination to force every new generation to accept society's traditional pattern of eating. To anyone with a responsible love for children or a concern with our blind repetition of habits that are leading our species further and further away from its evolutionary potentialities, the sight of the human young being compelled to adopt the dietary pattern of pigs and dingoes is one of the saddest spectacles of daily life.

It goes without saying that in the grossly unnatural world we have made for ourselves, even the most enlightened mother can have problems. Many Western women find they are unable to breast-feed at all. Time, availability of alternatives, orthodox pressures from relatives and clinics, these and other factors can make life a lot more complicated than the instinctive routine of the jungle, but while the responsible modern mother deserves every sympathy for her efforts to do the right thing, these factors increase rather than reduce her obligation to do all she can to make the transition from breast, dried or liquid cow's milk to solid foods as painless and natural as possible.

While it would be generalizing to say that all infants readily and in every circumstance accept the more natural changeover from breast milk to those nut creams mixed with pulped, sweet ripe fruits or honey, non-processed cereals, shredded raw root and leaf vegetables, dried fruits, etc., that give them all they need without the addition of any cow's milk, dairy products, meat, meat extracts or manufactured preparations, there is no doubt that the chances of 'transition tantrums' are greatly reduced by introducing children to the foods to which their chemistry was intended to respond. How odd, when one thinks about it for a moment, that we should ever have supposed otherwise! What can complicate matters is if they are already joined in battle with their mothers through being forced to accept the far less digestible cow's milk (intended by nature only for calves) and those tinned and packeted preparations that are at best a second-class substitute for the right natural food. To their lasting shame, some nutritionists have even shown such ignorance and irresponsibility as to suggest that the Battle of the Plate should be won by lacing each dish with white sugar, so further widening the gulf between the child and those natural fruits whence all needed sweetening can be derived. Once the pattern of persuasion, deceit and force is established, every subsequent stage can be fraught with difficulties. This is evidence only of the problems we have created for ourselves by centuries of bad habits; the absurdity of modern man is that most of us have to learn how to do what should come naturally – and not only in matters centred on the stomach, if the popularity of how-to-do-it sex books is anything to go by.

Most of us have long thought we know better than nature and are determined that our young should conform. So every orthodox book on child rearing plugs the necessity to introduce meat into an infant's diet as early as possible. By their own lights such authorities are at least being logical here; unless a child can be coaxed, bullied and bribed into eating meat early in life, he will seldom take to it after a decent interval of consuming food nearer to what his chemistry demands. Most such books take it for granted that infants have to be coaxed and cajoled to accept solids, as though this was a perfectly natural phenomenon. How many mothers, especially with their first child, have gone nearly demented with worry over the difficulty of getting enough food down the infant throat to cover a penny? There can be few parents in the so-called civilized world who do not know this to be so. Orthodoxy has for long been at pains to hide from them the reason why. Not rocking the boat is for most of us more important than knowledge of how best to rock the cradle. And the sad thing is that it is all so totally unnecessary.

Let us go a little further back in the light of the fact that even orthodox medicine often advises expectant mothers to reduce their consumption of meat, recognizing that flesh foods leave much to be desired in pregnancy.

For over thirty years the late Dr Cyril Pink, a foremost nutritionist, did work at the Stonefield Nursing Home that gave conclusive evidence that a vegetarian diet before childbirth is beneficial both to the child and its mother. Some 4,000 mothers were observed during pregnancy and were kept in touch with subsequently for ten or more years. Pink concluded that 'the ideal diet for pregnancy is not much different from that which is ideal for man and woman at other times. The principles are the same, but it is even more worthwhile to put them into practice. It is best to eat mainly fruit, salads, nuts and vegetables, with some cereal; at least half of the day's food should be taken fresh and uncooked.' In the absence of fruit and nuts, he suggested that dairy products and eggs be taken in moderation. Since Pink's day innumerable nutritionists, paediatricians and other specialists have learned the wisdom of his advice, and mothers put on a vegetarian diet, even shortly before the birth of their babies, have gained in health and exuberance. There has also been a marked tendency for earlier deliveries, many of these being without the help of anaesthetics.

The milk that a mother gives to her child when at the breast is a very special liquid, containing a unique balance of vitamins, minerals, proteins, carbohydrates and protective factors. It is mere common sense that the subsequent weaning period should introduce the child to a full adult diet via substances that chemically, and in texture and taste, bridge the gap between breast-milk and solids as gently and naturally as possible. It is nothing less than a form of violence to attempt to win children over to the toxic poisons, the coarse flavour and the unsympathetic texture of animal flesh. As Geofrey L. Rudd wrote in *Why Kill for Food?* '. . . it is only the persistence of the mother which overcomes this natural resistance to the first doses of meat and fish. The child becomes conditioned and finally accepts the nasty smells and tastes. In this way most of us become meat-eaters, not from choice but from early conditioning; it is only when our reasoning powers are developed that we can assess the possible advantages of an alternative diet, and by this time most of us are creatures of habit and just carry on.'

Writers more qualified than I have written on the health aspects of a vegetarian diet in childhood, but irrespective of the medical and statistical evidence (which seems entirely to support the argument of this book) I am convinced from lifelong observation of my own children (second generation vegetarians on their father's side) and those of both vegetarian and meat-eating friends, and now from my grandchildren, that not only are vegetarian children of healthy stock as physically fit, mentally alert and full of high spirits as any of their omnivorously reared contemporaries, but that in their complexions, in the incidence of childish complaints, in the gentleness of their natures and in their all-round air of well-being and general stability, the children who have followed the more natural eating pattern – provided it has been balanced and nutritionally sound – are ahead of the rest. The same, and perhaps more, must be said for children reared on a balanced vegan diet (see Chapter 7) – but that is not to say that an energetic vegan child may not imitate his gun-toting, space-invading peers until such time as, hopefully, his parents' influence proves stronger than that of school and society!

This is of course a generalization, and no generalization is entirely satisfactory. Factors other than diet invariably have to be taken into account. There are exceptions to every sweeping statement and it will be noted that I have inserted the qualification 'of healthy stock'. Much unfair criticism of vegetarian practice has been prompted by the observation of people who with some chronic illness or inherent constitutional weakness have after years of flesh-eating turned to vegetarianism, all too often as a last resort. For such unfortunates, or their children, to be judged as typical vegetarians or as evidence of the efficacy of a flesh-excluding diet, is of course absurd and unreasonable. Vegetarianism is not some miracle-working panacea, capable of reversing overnight the abuses or sicknesses of a lifetime. It is (or should be) part of a way of life from which most of us have departed with varying degrees of success or disaster. To regard it, as some do who occasionally submit to a fortnight's treatment on a health farm, as a kind of confessional for the body, guaranteed to cleanse the system prior to a further term of indulgence, is to get hold of the wrong end of a very frail stick.

Support for the argument that a natural diet is our right even before our birth could make this chapter far longer than it needs to be. Among other points that could be made is the fact that schools catering partly or entirely for vegetarian children have achieved impressive results in physical fitness, sporting records and academic results. But what says more than words or examples is that there is not a shred of evidence for a balanced vegetarian or vegan diet being *in*advisable for children of all ages; on the contrary, all the evidence supports the opposite – that the correct food from cradle to grave significantly increases the human being's chances of full health and vitality. While there is ample evidence that the consumption of meat carries danger for any frugivorous species, it is logical to assume that a natural diet must be innocent of any conceivable harm. *Argumentum ad judicium.*

However, meat is only one – though a large – part of an omnivorous human's diet and it is obviously not possible to pin on to any one substance the entire responsibility for a particular sickness, deficiency or reduction in vitality and well-being. It would be absurd to imagine that by eliminating just one item from our diet we can protect ourselves against all the consequences of our civilized eating patterns. The very best that most of us can do is to ensure that from childhood onwards we get as near as we can to the kind of food for which our bodies were designed.[1]

What deceives so many parents into accepting for their children substances about which a moment's rational thought would arouse the deepest doubt, is that all young animals are equipped by nature to withstand at least some of the vicissitudes of early life. Built into our very chemistry are safeguards against the hazards of the exploratory and growing period, so that substances which in adult years might well lay us low, can be to a lesser or greater degree absorbed without apparent harm when the tide of youth is running full and strong. Just as an apple tree that has its roots shortened by a careless ploughman or its bark stripped by sheep, will put out more blossoms than its unmolested neighbour, so nature rallies to ensure that when a species is threatened by war, disease, injury or other untoward circumstance, the maximum chance of survival is provided. As the tree strives for a heavier crop of fruit that will produce more seeds for self-perpetuation, in the same way the human or animal is given every opportunity to reproduce its kind, but nature is less concerned about what happens to it subsequently. Reproduction is given priority over longevity.

It follows, then, that the answer to our problems of over-population may well be seen to lie in our own ill-considered habits of life. The day may not be far away when we realize that the best method of keeping down our numbers is to continue to live our artificial and uninstinctive 'civilized' lives. Demographers and eugenists have already begun to suspect as much and the arrival of AIDS has done nothing to reduce that suspicion. But this is not really of much comfort to any concerned parent wanting for its child the best possible start in a life that will be presented with quite enough uninvited hazards and tensions without the added burden of self-induced mental, nervous or physical ill-health.

The bulk of reasonably intelligent parents are increasingly capable of looking at the white-faced, overweight and sickly children whose staple diet all too often consists of little but burgers, fish fingers, potato crisps, bottled sauces, useless mineral drinks, packets of harmful sweets and other worthless and additive-laden fillers and of drawing therefrom their own conclusions. The question they should feel obliged to ask themselves, however, is just how much better for their children is their own dietary pattern. (Sticking to the 'E-frees' is only part of the battle.)

This is something that can only be decided individually, but if in the light of what is being said parents are prepared to re-examine the whole question of their own and their children's daily food requirements, my purpose in writing this book will have been achieved. There is nothing greater we can give to those we love than the maximum opportunity to enjoy, and contribute usefully to, that life for which they did not ask and for which as parents we must take so much responsibility.

Notes

1. Among scientific research into the growth rates of children was that published in Albert von Haller's *The Vitamin Hunters* (Chilton, 1962), showing that vegetarian children have equal growth rates to that of children who consume a mixed meat and vegetable diet.

CHAPTER 5

Pathology or hygiene?

It is a vulgar error to regard meat in any form as necessary to life. All that is necessary to the human body can be supplied by the vegetable kingdom. It must be admitted as a fact beyond all question that some persons are stronger and more healthy who live on that (vegetarian) food. I know how much of the prevailing meat diet is not merely a wasteful extravagance but a source of serious evil to the consumer. I have been compelled by facts to accept the conclusion that more physical evil accrues to man from erroneous habits of diet than from even alcoholic drink.

Sir Henry Thompson, MD, FRCS, *Food and Feeding*

It (flesh food) is material which of malice aforethought has sedulously been rendered toxic during the animal's lifetime. In the first place his endocrine defences are interfered with by castration; he is then immobilized and over-fed, with a view to causing him to develop fatty degeneration of all his organs; and it is when this ugly process is complete that he is regarded as fit for human consumption.

Dr Leonard Williams, *The Practitioner*

The functioning of the mind is affected by food. There are certain kinds of food that supply the correct material for the activating of the mental process. Generally speaking, the mind works best on a mild diet, without meat and containing fresh vitamins and inorganic constituents rich in calcium phosphates. It requires an immense amount of nourishment, highly specialized and containing substances secreted by the endocrine organs of the body, which must, therefore, be in a generally healthy condition.

E. R. Rost, OBE, MRCS, LRCP,
The Nature of Consciousness

No physiologist would dispute with those who maintain that men ought to have a vegetable diet.

Dr Spenser Thompson

A certain amount has already been said in this book about the health aspect of a flesh-centred diet. Although I do not wish to over-stress this side of the argument – for I believe the case against meat-eating to reach far beyond the health of our own species – it does nevertheless come into the debate at several levels and must be given appropriate attention, even at the risk of repeating what has had to be said in other contexts elsewhere.

As Geoffrey L. Rudd has remarked, one of the remaining bastions against vegetarianism is the medical profession with its bias towards germs and chemicals. Although many doctors have at last joined the once-dreaded 'health lobby', orthodoxy still shows a profound reluctance to recognize the basic cause of ill health and, sadly, underrates the importance of diet. With their noses kept firmly to the grindstone of pathology, many doctors continue to be given a traditional training that perpetuates a fundamental misconception of disease and the process of healing. It is not pathology (the study of disease) but hygiene (the science of health) that will one day have to occupy our schools of medicine.[1] Apart from a passing – but thankfully growing – acquaintance with a few elementary diets for specific complaints, their curriculum excludes any serious study of the relationship between health and scientific nutrition. Undeniably, they are aided and abetted by most of their patients who would actually prefer to have organs removed than submit to self-discipline or common sense. All too many doctors and laymen appear eager for a panacea that will allow a continued disregard for the law of cause and effect. However, even the Government has come up with a 'Look After Your Heart' campaign, one of its members taking a lot of stick in 1987 for criticizing traditional diets.

Preventive medicine is still in its infancy and with the medical world dominated by the Molochs of the pharmaceutical industry whose profit-conscious concern is to promote a mounting reliance on an ever-widening range of powerful drugs, backed by constant high-pressure salesmanship, only the inarticulate sick have a vested interest in so unprofitable a condition as good health. Money may not be the root of all evil, but it unquestionably has a great deal to do with the path we have taken in pursuit of better health. Yet, although no one needs reminding today of the dangers of reliance upon medication that is founded on the empirical opportunism of the drug houses, we are all caught up in the spiral created by that folly and greed which have so often combined to make mankind its own worst enemy. The general practitioner, constantly got at, is more to be pitied than censured for his part in the conspiracy, caught as he is between the blandishments of the drug industry on the one hand, and the demands on the other of a public moving steadily away from first principles in its search for miracle cures that will enable them to go on living in the same bad old way.

No one would deny, of course, that some drugs have achieved striking, if not necessarily long-lasting, results. We are all glad of relief from pain or tension at times, even if the penalty for that relief is a wide range of side-effects and a reduction in our resistance to later disease. It is virtually impossible for any of us to avoid being caught up on the band-wagon of a health service that is founded on false principles, a remarkable ignorance of, or indifference to, alternative methods, and the stark and unwholesome realities of commercial enterprise. Though each of us may try to be an island, landing and embarkation points cannot be abolished. This, however, should increase rather than dis-courage our desire to arrive at the same and wider answers by means that are more truly scientific and founded not upon the barbarities of vivisection and animal research or on poisons that all too often merely repress symptoms and effect some seeming cures at the expense of lowered general health and resistance, but upon the sane and basic principles of good health. These are simple enough – that we should eat and live in the least artificial and stress-producing circumstances we possibly can. Nothing else can begin to bring us nearer to realizing the kind of health we must all want for ourselves and our children.

We have seen that a body, like an engine, needs the fuel for which it was designed. Fruits and nuts are the natural diet of man, as the instinctive inclinations of our children should alone be enough to show us without the scientific evidence that is so amply available, but, as this is the age of statistics and evidential data, it may be of interest to study some instances of the clear superiority of a vegetarian diet over meat in regard to health and endurance.

Among the studies that have taken place in developing regions of the world in an attempt to evaluate the diets and nutritional level of selected groups of people in rural areas, was one published in *The American Journal of Public Health* after a research team had visited Mexico. They reported that '. . . studies of the nutritional status of several population groups on the high plateau of central Mexico have demonstrated that the common dietary pattern is fundamentally sound. This pattern is based on a liberal consumption of tortillas, beans and chilli peppers, supplemented to a greater or lesser extent with foods obtained locally. The caloric intake is low and little animal protein is consumed.'

Not everyone wishes to subsist on tortillas, beans and chilli peppers, but all such examples of healthy and hardworked people being able to do so (and this is but one of many) have a cumulative value. A more recent study, undertaken in a remote Andean village by a medical research group from Harvard University and the University of Quito in Ecuador, found that many of the 400 townspeople over the age of fifteen lived to extraordinarily old ages. 'The oldest resident was a 121-year-old man. There were several over 100 years old and thirty-eight over the age of seventy-five. Of these thirty-eight, electrocardiogram studies were done on the twenty oldest, and only two showed any evidence of heart disease.' The article, which appeared in the *New York Times* on 22 April 1971, went on to say that Dr Campbell Moses, medical director of the American Heart Association, called the findings 'extraordinary' and said that such electrocardiogram studies of a similarly elderly population in the United States 'would show 95 per cent with cardiovascular disease'. It might be said that Dr Campbell Moses's amazement was much more extraordinary than the findings, which merely bear out facts that are well known and in line with what may be logically anticipated in the study of any group that is living as were these Andeans, on a basically pure vegetarian diet.

This example correlates with our knowledge of the Hunzakuts of Kashmir. Many accounts of these people have been given over the years, but one of the more impeccable pieces of orthodox information came from Major-General Sir Robert McCarrison, biochemist and physician to King George VI, who lived and worked with them in 1939. The Hunzakuts are known throughout the world for their longevity and freedom from disease. Their diet consists mainly of whole grains, fresh fruits, vegetables, goat milk and distinctly natural water. Their occasional indulgence in goat meat on feast days can hardly be taken into account. Dr McCarrison wrote: 'I never saw a case of asthenic dyspepsia, of gastric or duodenal ulcer, of appendicitis, or mucus colitis, or cancer . . . Among these people the abdomen over-sensitive to nerve-impressions, to fatigue, anxiety or cold was unknown.'

The Hunzakuts are perhaps nearer than most primitive people to Rousseau's over-idealized concept of the 'noble savage'. An erect, finely built people, as 'healthy as the wild fig tree' and tireless and fearless of old age and even death, they have done so well not merely on a diet that virtually excludes meat but on natural foods that, although of plant origin, are not by any means all that close to the preferred eating habits of the higher primates. Living as they do in the Himalayan passes, where fruits other than highly valued apricots are not plentiful, they have had to use their intelligence to conquer the poverty of nature in that part of the world. Sprouted cereals and legumes are important to them, for these are rich in the vitamins found in fruits, besides containing several times more of the B vitamins than do dry seeds. A turbid, yeasty beer is a further source of these vitamins. As might be expected, the Hunzakuts are very particular about the cereals they eat, tolerating none of the refined, white sloshy rice of the Indians. The coarse whole grains are used, complete with germ and fibre (bran), the proteins of refined cereals being inadequate for growth and the repair of human tissue. As is now well known, it is the germ of cereals, which is removed during refining, that contains the superior protein, for it is the germ that creates the new life, the rest of the seed or grain being merely a reservoir of energy – sugar tightly packed in the form of starch grains to take up less room. Much more could be said on these lines, but I do not wish to poach too far on the ground so well covered by writers who research into the refining processes and those other undesirable ways of tampering with food that are part and parcel of our artificial way of civilized life.

Another and much less documented group are the Tasaday people of Southern Mindanao in the Philippines, totally unknown to the outside world until their cave settlement in a seemingly impenetrable forest region was reached by a party of sociologists and anthropologists in the 1960s. Thought to have been cut off from communication for anything from 600 to 2,000 years, the Tasadays' way of life is (or was) that of the Stone Age, yet in no way supporting the glib popular concept of the club-swinging, steak-chewing, aggressive caveman. The Tasadays lack all belligerence. Their investigators found that small animals, birds, bats, insects and even venomous spiders shared their caves. It did not occur to the Tasadays to drive them out. As for the killing of animals for food, this was an unknown barbarism until the intrusion of a hunter from another tribe in 1966. It was this man, a southern Filipino, who forged the first link between the Tasadays and the outside world. He directed the expedition led by Manuel Elizalde, the Philippines' Presidential Adviser on National Minorities. The discovery of this small tribe of unknown people is, if authentic (and recent dubious journalism has sown doubts), another piece of evidence, if more were needed, to counter those anthropological theorists who claim that 'natural man' is a vicious, meat-eating predator.

By Western standards the Tasadays' diet is of course 'deficient'. They forage inside a radius of under three miles in the rugged, heavily-forested mountains that follow the general southeast-northwest axis of the Cotaboto coastline, eating wild fruit and large, pinkish flowers which are usually consumed on the spot. Before the Filipino hunter arrived, their staple food was a kind of wild yam, but the Filipino introduced them to *natek*, made from the starch and liquid that can be extracted from the pith of the palm tree and eaten either hot or (in the form of small cakes) cold. Raw or cooked palm cabbage is a frequent food, as are roasted green wild bananas. Although they catch and roast tadpoles, frogs, crabs and small fish, they do not even bother to eat the eggs of the birds which nest in their caves. If sickness comes they know instinctively which herbs may help recovery.

Although they lack salt and would appear to be limited in their diet by comparison with those arboreal primates who have a free run of the sun-reaching higher shoots and fruits that are available to the nippier species, the Tasadays were found to be in superb physical condition. The research team found only a few goitres and a single case of ringworm. Strictly monogamous, at childbirth only the wife and husband are present, the husband severing the umbilical cord and burying the placenta.

Until introduced to steel-bladed *bolos*, they used axes and other tools made from stone for such jobs as crushing the shell of the wild ginger fruit, hacking at banana stems and trunks, mashing betel nuts, pounding bark, splitting firewood, and so forth. Pebbles are split and rubbed against each other to make a cutting edge. Wooden knives, scrapers, digging sticks and fire-drills are their other main implements. But none of these is used for the sanguinary activities with which such tools have invariably been associated in our study of Stone-Age man. The Tasadays were found to be a loving and gentle people, lacking weapons and apparently any aggressive instincts. Greed is as unknown to them as real hunger. In scarcity the children are given priority, but the team found no clear structure of responsibilities and no apparent leadership.

What will happen – may already have happened – to the Tasadays is anyone's guess. Possibly the worst long-term threat comes from the logging companies, for the forest provides the Tasadays with all their necessities – their vegetarian food, their herbal medicines and the raw material from which they fashion their artefacts. The outlook is serious, not only for the Tasadays but for the whole range of cultural minorities that are known to be distributed throughout the archipelago, some of the groups being hardly more technically advanced than the Tasadays. It is greatly to be hoped that, without exploitation and interference with their lifestyle, information about such people will be more widely disseminated, for such living examples are a more powerful argument for the truth of man's natural diet than any number of fossilized bones – and fossilized theories.

Although their numbers are steadily eroded by the infiltration of Western habits, the peasants of many parts of the world follow a pattern that has much in common with the Hunzakuts and the Tasadays and has been little changed for centuries past. Coarse porridge, bread, thick vegetable soups, with in some cases meat featuring on ceremonial occasions – this has for long been the basic diet of many millions of the world's poorer populations. We do not have to follow so spartan a pattern, but if the inhabitants of parts of Bulgaria, Italy, Spain, southern Russia and elsewhere can experience robust health, boundless energy and often long life, on whole-grain cereals, fresh and sun-dried fruits and other plant foods, how little excuse have we to reject a similar routine when most of us can afford to add so many more tempting non-flesh items to such a diet?[2]

Research into flesh-excluding or flesh-reduced diets has also been undertaken in more economically advanced areas during times of national crisis. One such study took place in Denmark during the Allied Blockade of the First World War, when all imports were cut off. Realizing the possibility of acute food shortages, the government enlisted the advice of Denmark's vegetarian society and appointed Dr Mikkel Hindhede to direct its rationing programme. In 1920 Dr Hindhede discussed his project in the *Journal of the American Medical Association*:

> Our principal foods were bran bread, barley porridge, potatoes, greens, milk and some butter . . . the people of the cities and towns got little or no pork. Beef was so costly that only the rich could afford to

buy it in sufficient amount. It is evident, therefore, that most of the population was living on a milk and vegetable diet.

The results of this programme showed that the Danish people survived the war with improved health and lowered mortality rates. In the very first year of rationing, the mortality figures fell 17 per cent. In the year 1917-18, 6,300 fewer people died in Denmark than died in 1913, which was the previous year in which the mortality rate was lowest.

The *Journal of the American Dietetic Association* reported similar results from rationing in Norway during the Second World War:

> Norway had a similar experience during the war years of 1940-5 when it became necessary to make drastic cuts in the consumption of popular animal foods and increase the use of fish, cereals, potatoes and vegetables. Strom and Jensen (in *Mortality from Circulatory Diseases in Norway, 1940-5*) reported the favourable effect of this restriction on the mortality rate from circulatory diseases, as well as the prompt return to pre-war levels when the nation returned to its pre-war diet at the end of hostilities.

During the Second World War food rationing resulted, except where blockades or other exceptionally severe circumstances caused extreme quantitative inadequacy, in a notable increase in general health. This was not, of course, due only to the non-availability of animal foods, but also to the reduction in other (and particularly the refined and processed) foods.

Interesting and significant results came from a further nutritional study undertaken by Mervyn G. Hardinge, MD, of the College of Medical Evangelists in California, and Frederick J. Stare, MD, of Harvard University, as reported in the *Journal of Clinical Nutrition* in 1954.

In their study of 200 vegetarians and non-vegetarians these scientists observed only slight differences in physical measurement, blood pressures, and protein, albumin and globulin levels. The investigation included adolescents, pregnant women and adults between forty-five and seventy years of age. Each group was divided into (1) lacto-ovo-vegetarians (those who refrain from flesh foods but consume such animal products as milk and eggs), (2) pure vegetarians (vegans) and (3) non-vegetarians. Nutrient and caloric intakes were about the same for all groups.

Although laboratory and physical findings were similar in all groups, the pure vegetarians were found to weigh 20 pounds less than the others. The lacto-ovo-vegetarians and the non-vegetarians averaged 12 to 15 pounds above the ideal weight.

Weight gains and losses of pregnant women and average birth weights of infants, were similar in vegetarians and non-vegetarians. No evidence indicated that a vegetarian diet is insufficient for expectant mothers, nor did such a diet affect the growth rates of vegetarian adolescents who participated in the study. The report also found that 'there appears to be a tendency for the pure vegetarians to have mean corpuscular volumes somewhat higher than the lacto-ovo-vegetarians and non-vegetarians'. More recent data suggests that vegetarians and vegans have lower-than-average incidences of obesity, abnormal blood pressure and blood cholesterol; their intestines are in better condition and they are at lower risk of coronary heart disease, gallstones, kidney complaints and hormonally-related cancers.

The link between animal products (meat, eggs, butter, etc.) and numerous slight and severe forms of illness is sufficiently well known for even the most orthodox of medical text books to acknowledge the dangers and advise both the layman and his physician accordingly. To cite one example, steak eaten rare is helping to spread the virus salmonella, which causes acute food poisoning in adults, while uncooked meat has proved fatal to many young children. For the most part, however, such findings are presented so obliquely, so feebly and with so little follow-up that the implications are seldom realized.

Among the more firmly attested links is that between animal foods and those conditions caused by the deposition of sodium urate crystals in the body tissues, of which gout is one unpleasant example. Sodium urate, a salt of uric acid which is the end-product of purine metabolism, lodges beneath the skin or within the joints. This process produces the swellings and the hard white lumps that are a feature of this painful disease. As with so many other ills, orthodox medicine has concentrated chiefly on developing drugs with which to combat the symptoms rather than with propagating those abstinences which would remove the symptoms by removing the cause. However, because man and the apes are not adequately equipped by nature for dealing with the uric acid that is formed by the nucloproteins in which animal foods are especially rich, the relationship has not been overlooked by the more responsible authorities. Even as staid a popular reference book as *Black's Medical Dictionary* states flatly: '. . . inadequate exercise, a luxurious manner of living, habitual over-indulgence in animal food and rich dishes, and especially in alcoholic beverages, are undoubtedly important precipitating factors in the production of the disease.'

Medical opinion is divided as to whether an excessive intake of foods high in purines is the primary and essential *cause* of gout, for there is evidence that in the majority of cases the disease is primary (that is to say, of hereditary origin), but there is no general disagreement that animal food is an important precipitating factor. The red meats from hogs and cattle are particularly rich in purines, though such medical texts as J. L. Hollander's *Arthritis and Allied Conditions* (Lea & Febiger, 1966) instructs patients to avoid liver, sweetbread, brains, kidneys and all meat extractives, broth soups and gravies. That desk-shelf standby of British general practitioners, Sir Stanley Davidson's *The Principles and Practice of Medicine* (sixth edition, E. & S. Livingstone, 1963), advises that treatment should include diet 'of a vegetarian type', while Conybeare and Mann's medical 'bible' the *Textbook of Medicine*, although not excluding meat and fish in moderation, forbids absolutely Hollander's list of precipitating meat foods and adds fish roes and sardines for good measure, winding up with the advice that the diet should consist mainly of vegetables, bread, fresh fruit and cheese. One has only to read between the lines of such establishment texts as these, making due allowance for the fact that they take as their basis a pathological approach to health, a general under-valuation of diet in the treatment of disease and a growing dependence on drug therapy, to judge that if such authorities can go as far as they do in casting doubt or blame on animal foods, one may be pretty certain that their sorties in the direction of non-orthodox conclusions are marked more by under-statement than by its opposite.

When one turns to the evidence for a link between circulatory and heart disease and a diet based on animal foods, the case is even stronger and in less dispute. In 1961 an issue of the *Journal of the American Medical Association* stated that: '. . . a vegetarian diet can prevent 90 per cent of our thrombo-embolic disease and 97 per cent of our coronary occlusions.' As is widely known, high levels of cholesterol in the blood have been linked with increased chances of developing heart disease and no one seriously disputes that animal fats contribute powerfully to the presence of cholesterol in the human system. Referring again to the study made by Drs Hardinge and Stare, they confirmed that plant protein produces lower levels of cholesterol in the body than does animal protein and commented: 'The pure vegetarians had significantly lower serum cholesterol than either their lacto-ovo-vegetarian or non-vegetarian counterparts.'

A further study linking atherosclerosis[3] with meat eating was reported by William S. Collens, MD, a medical consultant at the Maimonides Medical Center in New York, and retired Clinical Professor of Medicine at the Downstate Medical Center in Brooklyn. In an article appearing in the December 1969 issue of *Medical Counterpoint* Dr Collens wrote:

> American men killed in the Korean war showed, even at the age of twenty-two, striking signs of arteriosclerotic disease in their hearts as compared with Korean soldiers who were free of this damage to their blood vessels. The Americans were well fed with plenty of milk, butter, eggs and meat. The Koreans were basically vegetarians.

Among other scientific researchers to have explored the effect of a vegetarian diet on blood circulation in humans is Dr Oxford Muller, inventor of the capillary microscope. He explained that 'The influence of a vegetable diet presents itself in this way: the capillaries stretch out and their convolutions become straightened out. We thus can see that this form of nourishment causes a certain unburdening of the peripheral section of the blood vessels while the purely meat diet seems to represent a heavy burden.' (*The Vitamin Hunters* by von Haller, Chilton, 1962.)

Almost exclusive to human beings, atherosclerosis and such associative conditions as angina pectoris are marked by the presence of plaques of fatty-protein material which contain the cholesterol. Unlike many other animals, humans are able to manufacture cholesterol without the substance being present in their diet, and this is one reason why it is widely held that foods containing large amounts of cholesterol (notably animal fats, including dairy products and eggs) may be a major factor in the development of atherosclerosis. The arterial walls, it is held, accumulate fats derived from the circulating blood that has itself drawn on the cholesterol-rich foods that have been consumed by the affected subject. This has been experimentally supported by the research done on rabbits which, when fed on large amounts of fats, develop these plaques. In world-wide surveys on humans it has been established almost without exception that people with the lowest animal-fat consumption have the lowest incidence of atherosclerosis. After the Second World War certain sections of the Japanese people whose former diet consisted largely of seafood and rice and whose incidence of coronary artery disease was very low, began to eat Western foodstuffs. Some years later it was found that the incidence of coronary artery disease in these people had approached that of the Americans who had introduced them to their more sophisticated and unnatural way of eating.

It is well known that fat people are more prone than thin to atherosclerosis and that there is an inverse relationship between undernutrition and the disease. It was found after the last World War that grossly undernourished subjects showed signs of only trivial atherosclerosis and in many cases the condition was altogether absent.

Not only has it been conclusively shown that a reduction in the cholesterol level results from a diet that is deliberately kept low in animal fats, but it is also known that if someone with a high blood level of cholesterol accepts a diet rich in unsaturated fats (e.g., the vegetable oils), a distinct lowering of the blood cholesterol is likely. Business executives in the United States, alarmed by their first heart attack, have taken to drinking massive quantities of sunflower seed oil daily in the hope of arresting their atherosclerosis. Quite apart from the unpleasantness of such a drastic 'remedy' (for hefty flavouring is necessary to make such large neat quantities palatable), so unbalanced an attempt to restore the equilibrium is neither scientific nor, possibly, wise. Their more sensible course would be to adopt a diet more natural to their species, but the main hope, as always, is more likely to lie with estrogens, anti-coagulants and dilatatory drugs, although the dangers in all such unsatisfactory measures are well known to the medical profession and would not be considered for a moment in a society that had not reached lunatic heights in its perverse refusal to face the absurdly simple answer to so many of its health problems, namely that prevention is infinitely preferable to any hoped-for cure. However, prevention is at last being taken more seriously.

With almost half the deaths in the United States being due to arterial disease, marked by a steady and alarming increase of ischaemic heart disease in all classes, but especially in the working class, in men under forty-five and in women over the age of fifty-five years (see Davidson: *The Principles and Practice of Medicine*), the arteriosclerotic diseases comprise one of the major killers of our species. It has been established that not only animal fats, but also protein intake, have to be considered in relation to the pathogenesis of atheroma. The whole picture gets somewhat technical if one explores it in depth, but the facts are available in most of the established medical works as well as in the more popular presentations, so none of us need be in ignorance of the risks we take in persisting with foods that any hyena, but clearly not man, can take in its stride.

Unfortunately, even though one in four British men aged 35 will have suffered a coronary 'event' before they retire, such is our species' detestation of change that the vast (but perhaps decreasing) majority need such overwhelming proof that their lifestyle is inadvisable, that most of them are dead or chronically sick before they can accept what is obvious to anyone prepared to study available findings objectively. 'But it has not been absolutely proved!' is the kind of cry that is heard so often from the ranks of the habit-stricken. No one in his right mind could today suggest that it has not been 'proved' that smoking can actually cause lung cancer, yet up go the consumption figures, hotly pursued by the cancer statistics, and still there are plenty of people to be heard protesting that 'Only a *relationship* has been established.' It is all a little like saying that when an unarmed man is pushed into the cage of a starving, tormented, but still robust tiger, there is no proof that the latter will eat the former, because their juxtaposition is evidence of nothing more than a 'relationship'.

As a final word on the heart and circulatory diseases, it is not being denied that stress of all kinds is contributory. There is no doubt whatsoever that arterial disease is particularly prevalent in countries with a high standard of material living. To what extent the strains of modern (and particularly urban) life and the abuses of smoking, alcohol and the processing of foods are responsible, can of course be argued until the cows come home, but as atherosclerosis appears to be responsible for more disability and death than any other disease and is the cause of death in almost all heart attacks and about half the deaths from strokes and sugar diabetes, the very considerable contribution made by animal fats to the pathogenic picture can only be ignored by those determined to live in cloud-cuckoo land.

The other great killer of Western man is cancer. Innumerable authorities have been at pains to point out that the increasing medication of animal feeding stuffs that is the result of our economic rat race and the heartless profit-chasing that has produced 'factory farming', means we are likely to be swallowing antibiotics in our milk, arsenic and sulfa-drug residues in our bacon and pig's liver, and, until their recent banning in the EEC, USA and UK, the cancer-causing female hormone-analogue diethylstilbestrol in those flannel-like slabs of tasteless chicken so inexplicably one of the symbols of the Western *dolce vita*. With Europe already surfeited with over-production of meat and milk, drugs, hormones, and now probiotics are being used to boost productivity, fertility and fecundity, driving livestock to the brink of physiological breakdown. One bovine growth hormone is under test to boost the cow's output of milk by some 20 per cent, such is the insanity of those profit-seekers who would turn the milk lakes into ever deeper lochs.

Regardless of the many hazardous substances that are injected into animals in the pursuit of greater profits and in the hope of combatting the ever more threatening diseases that factory farming and other unnatural methods of stock care bring about, suspicion has been directed at meat itself as a contributory or even causative source of cancer. Pathogenic bacteria are splashed from urine and faeces in the slaughter-house onto the flesh. They may also be transmitted by the dirty habits of slaughterers and others. Meat causes four out of five cases of food-poisoning in the UK. Cooking – all through the meat – can kill most of the bacteria, but raw meat can spread disease in kitchens, on working surfaces, etc. Shellfish may transmit poisons not destroyed by cooking.

Decomposition begins as soon as an animal is slaughtered. Its bloodstream, just like our own, serves as a debris conveyor for toxic wastes. After death these wastes are added to by the natural process of disintegration, involving bacterial organisms which can proliferate every fifteen minutes at body temperature, causing over 90 per cent of all recorded cases of food poisoning. Cooking is not enough to remove the toxicity, and the germs which develop on pre-cooked meat and fish can be even more deadly. To give our system the additional job of eliminating another creature's unwanted material together with the toxins of fear that are released into its bloodstream prior to slaughter, seems to suggest, at the least, a very unaesthetic regard for the joys of nutrition. As is widely known, domesticated animals suffer from innumerable diseases – not only from cancer but also from tuberculosis, contagious abortion, swine fever, foot and mouth, mastitis and a host of others – and it would be naïve indeed to suppose that all diseased meat is detected and fed to our pets instead of to us.

The dangers from unpasteurized milk have required severe restrictions on its sale. Liquid egg is another notorious source of salmonella. Abuse of antibiotics in farming, especially in the nefarious marketing of very young calves, has led to the spread of highly resistant organisms and compromised medical applications of antibiotics.

To what extent human cancers can be attributed to these repellant facts of animal exploitation has yet to be confirmed, but the statistics are reason enough for concern. Epidemiologists attribute 35 to 50 per cent of all cancer deaths to dietary causes; in 1970, in the United Kingdom alone, there were 117,085 cancer deaths, against a mere 26,721 in 1900. An alarming increase, making all allowance for population increase and any advances in detection. After bronchial carcinoma, cancer of the large bowel is the most common cause of death from cancer and the one most often associated with flesh eating.

As with arterial diseases, cancer is predominantly a disease of the affluent nations and it is the second commonest cause of death among children. Despite the tens of millions of animals that are sacrificed in the research laboratories every year, cancer is also one of the most rapidly increasing diseases. If instead of groping for cures in the tormented entrails of friendly dogs, as Shaw so graphically put it, scientists had directed their minds towards disseminating a preventive programme based on saner and less self-indulgent living, untold misery might have been spared all species involved in the whole hideous canvas of suffering that is the penalty of our civilized folly.

As has been stressed by Dr Francis Roe, Research Co-ordinator to the Tobacco Research Council, one-time senior lecturer in Cancer Research at the London Hospital Medical School and later Reader in Experimental Pathology at the Chester Beatty Institute of Cancer Research, so far from the causes of cancer not being known, as some have claimed, all too many causes have been traced of all too many varieties of the disease. Certain drugs, food contaminants, X-irradiation and environmental pollutants (tobacco, industrial wastes, etc.) are among the unquestioned causes. Such admissions from the bastions of orthodox medicine might get us all somewhere if they were backed by signs of a more fundamental concern for preventive measures and true hygiene. Instead, hope continues to be placed in such empirical measures as ever more sophisticated drugs and in the field of molecular biology. The concern is too much with how we can continue to do all the things that produce our diseases, yet somehow manage to cheat nature's responses.

Even those most concerned with not rocking the boat by implicating the follies of our modern way of life are agreed that cancer is not a single disease with a single cause, but a reaction of the tissues to a variety of exciting agents. 'Foreign bodies' – that is to say, substances which the human organism is not equipped by nature to accept and absorb – are unquestionably a major cause of malignant growths. While we may lack the kind of evidence that will satisfy scientific criteria that meat (a distinctly 'foreign body' in more than one sense) can actually create a cancerous condition in the human 'grave' in which it becomes buried, the knowledge at our disposal makes it quite absurd to doubt the strong possibility. By the exaggerated standards of proof some diehards demand, even today, tobacco smoking must also be dismissed as a cause of cancer. Yet, at long last, it has officially and widely been pronounced that smoking does quite evidently cause the disease, though for years this was a suggestion dismissed as cranky overstatement by those who never wish to face the promptings of common sense that so often become the hallowed scientific fact of tomorrow. An immense number of lives must have been lost, not only due to smoking, while we have hung around waiting for the experts to confirm what many reasonably clear-minded laymen had long ago seen to be the result of putting two and two together.

Irrespective of the fact that various substances cause or (if the cautious prefer) predispose to, cancer,[4] it makes more than mere 'sense' to suspect the role of meat than it does to dismiss it – especially in view of the undoubted fact that in the Western world today it is virtually impossible to eat the flesh of any animal, bird or fish without ingesting unnatural substances that the creature has itself taken into its system (sometimes with considerable cumulative results) through the food chain that links all species.

It is widely agreed that high-protein feeding speeds the rate of spread of cancers in experimental animals, and scientists have shown conclusively that cancer runs parallel to the incidence of overeating as measured by calories. It would be foolish to doubt, rather than foolish to suppose, that animal foods, full of growth hormones and growth stimulants, contribute to the madness of the cancer cell. As the 'rich man's disease', cancer (long before the invention of chemical additives) was known as the Royal Rot, as it occurred in so many monarchs and those who could afford to eat the most expensive (animal) foods. The privileged classes have always been particularly prone to cancer and other degenerative disease and as soon as such foods became available to the mass of the people, these diseases no longer knew any class barriers and descended upon rich and relatively rich alike. At least in days gone by our ancestors ate animals and birds that had fed on uncontaminated food grown on wholesome land. For the peasantry, meat was a garnish to essentially vegetarian fare. Offal, low in fat, were made into pasties, etc. – hence umbel pie, later gentrified to 'humble pie'. Hunted animals and culls of draft beasts (e.g., oxen) would have been low in fat, and the fat lower in saturated fats than in today's domesticated species. Resultant ill health may well have had more to do with excessive consumption than with parallels to the chemical hazards that are now in virtually every mouthful of flesh our species consumes. Nothing is likely to equal the sheer quantitative suffering we inflict on other creatures, but it is perhaps not fanciful to say that in our cancers and many other ills we may be experiencing that 'fruit' of *karma* that we have done so much to deserve by our unceasing indifference to the rights of the animal kingdom.

Pain and the subnormal functioning of the human body are nature's first warning that something is wrong and, as the vast majority of our physical problems are attributable to faulty living – and particularly to an unbalanced diet far removed from the simple raw, fresh fruits, nuts and other plant life on which we evolved for millions of years – it is inexcusable that the bulk of medical research is still devoted to the discovery of new drugs to obliterate and suppress symptoms, driving deleterious matter back into the bloodstream, instead of advocating the cleansing of the body's arteries by pouring pure substances into them in place of the effluents of our modern living. In these days of cellular biology and pharmacology's concentration on discovering causes of disease and devising selective interventions, these images may sound old fashioned, but the point is valid. If you tip sewage and industrial waste into a river you create a sick and dying stretch of water. To create healthy conditions you do not dose a river with drugs. You stop pouring muck into it. Why should we treat our bodies differently? In point of fact we treat them even more badly than our rivers, for in refusing to avoid the primary cause of so much of our ill health, and in adding to the accumulated toxins the further poisons of the drugs with which we hope to nullify the consequences of our abuses, we all too often find that the subsequent reactions of our bodies are even more violent and need ever more powerful drugs to give a further illusion of improvement.

As hardly needs saying, all organs from the brain to the kidneys may be seriously affected by drugs, whatever the reason is for them having been administered. The final result may be long delayed because the body has great resistance, but there is bound to be a degree of damage because no organism is meant to have toxic materials introduced orally or intravenously. Their introduction places a burden on the organs of elimination, upsets the intestinal flora, the natural bacteria and the nervous sytem. It would take a lot of wishful thinking to dispel the connection between the fast-rising incidence of nervous disorders and the vast daily bombardment of our bodies by the wide range of pharmaceutical products that have become part and parcel of modern life. The link between specific drugs and vaccines, and diseases such as tuberculous meningitis, and a wide range of physical and nervous disorders, has too often been suggested to merit further attention here. My aim is merely to stress once again that it is surely infinitely more scientific and commonsensical to treat our bodies in such a way that the need to call upon drugs of any kind is done away with or at least reduced to an absolute minimum. It is madness and often suicide, as all good doctors agree, to court ill health by embracing without conscious reservations and abstentions a lifestyle that is virtually certain to have repercussions by upsetting our bodily chemistry.

The question of human health cannot be divorced from the ethical aspect of our reliance upon drugs and vaccines. Quite apart from the appalling fact that the first children to be inoculated with a new vaccine are nothing less than human guinea pigs, anyone with an iota of compassion should be concerned that untold thousands of monkeys – highly sensitive creatures whose 'human' reactions and pleasures are often pathetically akin to many of our own – have had to sacrifice their kidneys for the manufacturing processes, yet more thousands having their living brains injected with the vaccine to test each batch for virulence. As Geoffrey Rudd has rightly remarked, 'anything so utterly barbarous, selfish and devilishly wrong in principle could not be right in practice' – a point of view that only those totally sold on the humanistic scientific argument can possibly rebut. The fact that polio vaccine is now produced in less exceptionable ways offers only limited cause for congratulation. Once science is divorced from moral considerations, we have opened the door to any depth of brutality and evil – a realization so persuasively and brilliantly argued by the microbiologist Dr Catherine Roberts in her book *The Scientific Conscience*.

The picture is not a happy one. Heart troubles, constipation, ulcers, varicose veins, migraines, obesity, diverticulitis, diabetes, some cancers and many other ills and imbalances, both physical and nervous, are increasing at an alarming rate. Millions of pounds are poured into research, yet hardly any of it into the investigation of diet. We take it quite for granted that this should be the case, though even medical journals have begun to suggest that somewhere along the line medicine may have taken a wrong turning. If the rivers of medicine which we pour into our long-suffering systems were one quarter as effective as their pushers try to make us believe, we would be living in surroundings that more closely resembled the Elysian Fields than a vast out-patients department. The crowding in hospitals and waiting rooms and the vast sums of money spent on treating established disease, are not a testimony to progress and modern healing methods, but a thundering admission of our abysmal failure to understand the foundation of disease or to cope with its result.

However, there are shafts of hope. An editorial in the *British Medical Journal* as long ago as 29 January 1972, was able to state that:

> Nutrition is taught to medical students as fag-ends of physiology, biochemistry, clinical medicine and paediatrics . . . The day is past in Britain when Edward Mellanby could change the physique of the nation with some spoonfuls of cod-liver oil. We now have to begin to learn the more subtle relationships that exist between nutrition and medicine and how changes in food habits and changes in food production may affect health. Medical education must keep pace with the rapid advances in this subject.

Some doctors have been more outspoken and explicit than this. Robert Blomfield, MB, ChB, of St Stephen's Hospital, Chelsea, for instance, wrote flatly (*Sunday Times*, 10 June, 1973): 'The fact is that the medical profession in this country has in general largely ignored the role of diet in the causation of disease, the emphasis being on the treatment of established disease when the damage has been done.' After condemning refined sugar and white bread – that 'bleached, softened, chemical-ridden, protein and vitamin depleted imitation of the real thing (whole wheat bread)' – he goes on:

> Most people buy what the advertisers tell them to as they, and the doctors who should be advising them, know no better. One has only to sample the average hospital meal to see how low on the list of priorities food comes in modern medicine. What is urgently needed is the widespread realization that you are what you eat and drink and breathe and that if these factors deviate far from nature trouble/illness will ensue to a greater or lesser extent. If a fraction of the money spent on research into the treatment of disease was used to investigate the relationship of diet to disease, the health of people in this country could be dramatically improved across the board, but much of this research is financed by drug companies who have a vested interest, not surprisingly, in drug treatment. And if one looks at it closely, so have most doctors. Naturally grown unprocessed foods . . . are the basis of all good health – but, amazingly, this fundamental factor is almost, if not completely, neglected in British and American medical schools, where science rules the roost, as in our hospitals where investigations and therapeutic firework displays are the order of the day. There is an old Chinese saying 'Medicine is used when nutrition has failed.' No

wonder the pharmaceutical industry, which spends roughly £300 a year for each doctor in this country on promoting its products, is doing so well!

Concerned about over-nutrition in children, Dr Barry Lewis, director of the lipid disorders clinic at Hammersmith Hospital, London, has emphasized that dietary prevention of heart disease should begin in childhood, research having shown that in the coronary-prone Wester-nized countries newborn boys have thicker walls to their coronary arteries than those born in relatively immune populations. The next stage, the depositing of fat in the artery walls, could begin during the first ten years of life. Dr Lewis also added his voice to those who have warned of the very high saturated (blood-cholesterol-raising) fat content of cow's milk produced by modern farming techniques. There have been several indications of late that milk is at last being seen for what it is – a grossly over-valued commodity within any society where there is an adequacy of other nutrients. The almost hysterical over-selling by the dairy industry will doubtless continue for so long as this chemical-ridden fluid – in its pure state intended only for calves – is the by-product of an over-productive meat industry. Various factors can affect the situation[5] and, because less affluent nations get little of this surplus, there is now a growing interest in the development of plant milks. Where a cow gives as milk only about one tenth of the protein she eats, mechanical processing can raise that fraction to 75 per cent, the milk being derived directly from lucerne grass, vegetables, palm and sugar cane leaves, soya beans, rice stalks, pea pods and other crop residues. As has been suggested earlier, such techniques should make enormous contributions to eliminating malnutrition in undeveloped countries, providing a nourishing liquid containing none of the dangers inherent in the normal 'pinta'.

Milk is not the only idol to take a knock recently. Even the belief long held by former 'cranks' that roughage is an essential part of a healthy diet is getting strong support from the medical profession. Many diseases are now suspected of being the result of too little rough fibre, including bowel cancer and even coronary thrombosis. Until recently conventional medical wisdom advocated a highly refined 'low residue' diet for diverticular diseases (suffered by 20 per cent of Western people over forty years old) on the grounds that roughage irritated the bowel. Now these sufferers and far greater numbers of people who have constipation are being told by more enlightened doctors to take such natural foods as wheat bran. Even a raw cabbage stalk has been seen to have its place in the scheme of things.

Mr Denis Burkitt, a surgeon who spent many years in Africa before being employed by the Medical Research Council, has pointed out that rural Africans who eat bulky fibrous foods rarely suffer from constipation, bowel cancer and appendicitis, whereas city Africans and American Negroes who eat refined foods and often far more meat, suffer from them as do whites. Burkitt's view that chemicals manufactured by bacteria in stagnant stools remaining in the intestines for long periods may cause cancer and that the presence of roughage encourages the development of a healthier bacterial flora, ties in with what a lot of 'fringe' investigators have suspected for some time. It is also significant that coronary heart disease and gallstones, both linked with a high blood cholesterol (gallstones are often formed from solidified cholesterol), are far less frequently found in people with a proper intake of roughage.

In 1972 one clinical investigation provided convincing evidence that unprocessed wheat bran will prevent much bowel trouble. Mr Neil Painter, senior surgeon at Manor House Hospital, reported that sixty-two out of seventy patients with diverticular disease experienced marked relief of symptoms and a regular bowel habit, without need to strain on passing a stool, after taking a bran diet. The majority of patients formerly had to take laxatives but were able to give them up.

If these examples are not enough to show that even orthodox medicine's attitude to the unscientific and emotional opposition to the diet natural[6] to our species has become tinged with impatience, in 1973 the new family health encyclopaedia *Mind and Body* (Orbis Publishing Limited, 1973), under the heading 'Vegetarianism', presented an up-to-date admission that its profession was still lagging behind the facts. After suggesting that if it is more healthy to be a vegetarian this is probably because indirectly it may result in eating *less* (a startling about-face from the extraordinary statement quoted in Chapter 6 from *Black's Medical Dictionary* of an earlier decade), the article continued:

> Undeniably it is more 'natural' to be a vegetarian, in that for the majority of people during most of man's history, meat has been a rare item of the diet and vegetarianism an economic necessity ... Even medical authorities often insist that vegetarianism is unhealthy and veganism certain to result in dietary deficiencies. The evidence does not support these assertions. Careful studies have shown that the most likely deficiencies to occur – vitamin B_{12} and iron – are not found in even strict vegans. No doubt this can be attributed to the fact that all vegetarians are careful with their diet and take care to avoid dietary deficiencies. However, this does not detract from the point. Careless vegetarians, like careless meat eaters, can eat a poorly balanced diet,

but a rational approach to nutrition avoids these problems. Another invalid objection that is often used by their opponents is that vegetarians are likely to become protein deficient. The assiduous use of nuts by many vegetarians is an attempt to avoid this deficiency. However, such attempts are not needed, because protein comprises a considerable proportion of the calories in normal vegetables. If a vegetarian eats enough food (even without nuts) he will get enough protein.[7]

Although *Mind and Body* takes the view that the case for vegetarianism rests on moral and aesthetic grounds, their dismissal on scientific grounds of some of the sillier objections to a humane diet is a most encouraging indication of the way the wind is blowing. It may be deduced from other articles in the encyclopaedia that this light breeze of change has been influenced by the realization that a humane diet is fast becoming an ecological priority.

Although such suggestions and findings as these would have been regarded as wildly heretical and way out a few years ago, we are still a long way from seeing general orthodox acceptance of the paramount necessity to study nutrition in the light of human physiology and the facts of comparative anatomy. The time is coming, beyond a doubt, if only for the reason that the economic and ecological problems the world has to face will in time make a virtue of necessity. That Governments themselves are showing concern is encouraging – though one Edwina Currie doesn't make a summer.

There must, however, be a balance in all this. In vegetarianism we have but one aspect, though a most important one, of what may one day be recognized as an altogether better and more mature way of life. As things are, and in view of the many other abuses which none of us can avoid entirely, it must be accepted that vegetarianism cannot guarantee the cure or prevention of every bodily ill, but it is reasonable and wholly scientific to believe that in a natural and considered diet we have a better long term chance of eliminating much ill health and creating a bodily chemistry that can better resist the many stresses and impurities it is impossible to avoid.

There is of course a place for modern medicine and surgery, even a place for certain drugs of plant origin (all animals know instinctively which herbs they need when feeling below par, and the human science of herbalism is far too often written off as a cranky specialism by those whose own remedies are far more suspect). It would be foolish to suggest that nothing of value has been learned from orthodox medicine, whose age-long concerns have reached beyond the sadly empirical, negative and commercially-controlled methods that unfortunately are the hallmark of so much modern research, but we really no longer have any excuse for ignoring the implications of that wider knowledge of so many relevant and related matters that we have today. A humane (and therefore automatically more natural) diet is just one part of the new ecological understanding that has awakened in recent years. The diet natural to man is one of the most important priorities of our time, but it is only part of the new, more holistic concept of our world and our place therein which I believe is being seen more clearly, especially by younger people sickened and alarmed by the environment they have inherited.

It is evident on all sides that thinking young people are increasingly opposed to the carnage and brutality on which Western society has been founded. It would be an overstatement, or at least an oversimplification, to suggest that all the gore-bespattered pages of our history books can be traced to the meat that has irritated and inflamed the human blood-stream, but there is little doubt that it has played a significant part. The decomposition of animal proteins in the unsuitably long gut of our species creates poisons that affect both mind and body. All other factors being equal, vegetarians are second to no meat eater in strength, stamina, good health and longevity, but the suggestion has more than once been made that actual aggression – that misdirection of the energy that is natural to all healthy organisms – is more likely to be instigated by the latter than by the former. It would probably be profitless to pursue this idea, for examples in support and denial would be legion, but on many counts the eating of animal foods can fairly be judged as the most pernicious Ice Age habit that human beings have yet to break. The savage, hunting energetically and helping his body to burn out the poisons, gets away with much more than sedentary, toxic, civilized man. As F. A. Wilson has said:

> For purely economic reasons many human beings gave up eating the flesh of animals when the Ice Ages ended, but recently the industrialization of the food industry has enabled animal foods, previously the privilege of only the rich, to be eaten daily by the average man, and so modern man has literally eaten his way back to the Ice Ages through the carcases of beasts. As the cause of mental and physical sin, no wonder meat stands out with the redness of blood. Man pays for the sin of unnecessary slaughter by the slaughter of his own kin; the revenge for the horror of the slaughter-house is the battlefield.

To the battfield might well be added the hospital ward. Wild exaggeration? I believe not. The time may not be far off when man will look back with amazement at the day when in our ignorance, our selfishness and our cruelty we had the arrogant impertinence to suppose that we were clever enough to cheat ourselves and our environment, not only by eating like indiscriminate jackals, but in seeing no argument other than the supremacy of violence, no virtue save the extension of greed, and no future except in the continuation of habits and thought patterns which Later Man may see to have been futile and destructive of the very balances and principles that 'civilization' should have stood for. Can he, in time, find the maturity to reverse such manifestations of his self-indulgence and arrogance as AIDS and genetic engineering?

Notes

1. Therapeutics (defined as any system that attempts to cure disease without removing the cause) is not only the province of orthodox medicine. Most specialisms need to aim higher than the mere suppression of symptoms. The rules of natural hygiene make far more sense than most healing theories, though like all methods it cannot by itself solve every problem of the psycho-physical organism, any more than can acupuncture, osteopathy, herbalism, etc., valuable though each of these can be in the appropriate circumstances. The body's natural condition is health. Disease is the body's reaction to neglect or abuse. We have for too long lost sight of this fundamental truth.

2. At this stage it should be firmly stressed that at no point is it being suggested that anything but an *adequate* vegetarian diet is being advocated. To quote nutritionist F. A. Wilson again: 'Only when man's typical plant foods are the mainstay of the diet – fruits first of all in abundance, then shoots, green and tender and full of vitamins and first-class protein, whole seeds by preference germinated, nuts and other vegetables, eaten raw as much as possible and grown on a really healthy soil – can a vegetarian [vegan would be a more correct term. JWT] diet outdo the mixed one. A vegetarian diet of over-boiled foods, insufficient fruits and tender greens, with refined flour and other mush is very inferior to a 'mixed' [i.e., including dairy products] diet.' So let there be no misunderstanding on this point. It is no good for anyone merely to give up both meat and dairy products and expect to sail along in better or even equal health on an ill-considered alternative diet. Although there is no risk in adopting a wholesome diet that includes a modest quantity of cheese and milk and totally excludes meat, if both meat *and* dairy products are excluded it is essential that alternatives be provided. A chapter on veganism follows.

3. Atherosclerosis means, literally, 'hardening of the arteries'. It covers three distinct conditions, *arteriosclerosis* (occurring in the smaller arteries in raised blood pressure), *medical sclerosis* (in certain arteries to muscles) and *atherosclerosis* (the most common by far and affecting the lining of the larger distributing arteries of the body).

4. Some spices, for instance, are injurious and are considered responsible for gastric ulcers and even cancer in Indians.

5. In the year 1972/3, in response to Government, total sales in the UK rose by 15 million gallons to top the 95-million-gallon rise in the previous twelve months, but by early 1974 the price of feeding stuffs had risen dramatically and milk production slumped badly. Quotas are at present operating on milk production in the EEC, and low-input systems are being investigated.

6. The question of how 'natural' specific plant foods are for man is a study in itself. Are oranges 'natural' for those who live in cold climates? Did prehistoric man's migration from warmer regions deprive our species of instinctively chosen foods, without which we uninstinctively adapted to alternatives (not only meat) for which chemically and physiologically we were (and may have remained) unsuited? Should we consume 'natural' foods only when they are in season and natural to the region and hemisphere we live in? We must not be over-complacent when we speak of 'natural foods'. It can be a relative term.

7. Since the last edition of this book, Britain's epidemic of diet-induced premature degenerative disease has prompted the Government to recommend a reduction of fat-intakes by one eighth and an increase of dietary fibre by a half. It will take more than juggling with low-fat milk and lean 'hormonized' meat to fulfil these recommendations, and doctors are entertaining ideas for healthy and prudent diets that entail an early vegetarian trend to much increased consumption of vegetables, fruit and unrefined cereals and pulses, with corresponding reductions of meat-consumption by as much as 70 per cent. These recommendations are founded on living proof from studies in Britain and elsewhere that vegetarians 'wear better': they suffer less from obesity, disorders of the intestines and circulatory system and from stones in the kidneys and gall-bladder. A vegetarian diet is rich in protective factors that seem to ward off prevalent threats, such as cancer of the breast and colon, associated with heavy consumption of animal products. Degenerative diseases set in later on in the lives of vegetarians, who occupy less than normal attention from doctors and in hospital and take less time off work.

CHAPTER 6

Values in perspective

Flesh foods are not the best nourishment for human beings and were not the food of our primitive ancestors. There is nothing necessary or desirable for human nutrition to be found in meats or flesh foods which is not found in and derived from vegetable products.

Dr J. H. Kellog

Comparative anatomy and physiology indicate fresh fruits and vegetables as the main food of man.

Dr S. M. Whitaker, MRCS, LRCP,
Man's Natural Food: An Enquiry

That it is easily possible to sustain life on the products of the vegetable kingdom needs no demonstration for physiologists, even if the majority of the human race were not constantly engaged in demonstrating it, and my researches show not only that it is possible, but that it is infinitely preferable in every way.

Alexander Haig, MD, FRCP

It must be honestly admitted that, weight for weight, vegetable substances, when they are carefully selected, possess the most striking advantages over animal food in nutritive value . . . I should like to see the vegetarian and fruit-living plan brought into general use, and I believe it will be.

Sir Benjamin W. Richardson, MD, FRS

It seems clear from the work of the past ten to fifteen years that the mutually supplementary effect of the proteins from cereals, roots and leafy vegetables is such as to provide an excellent amino blend for tissue construction and maintenance. Of course, we should have realized this quite clearly from the records of vegetarian people which are quite convincing in this respect.

Sir Jack C. Drummond, late Professor of Biochemistry,
London University, Harben Lecture, 1942

There are many alternative sources of first-class protein and the meatless diet can be as good as any other.

Dr Charles Hill, PC, MA, MD, DPH, LLD, Parliamentary
Secretary to the Ministry of Food 1951-5, the first Armstrong
Memorial Lecture, 1951

I do not eat flesh, fish or fowl. I drink neither the narcotics which are used as stimulants (alcohol mostly) nor the true stimulants like tea . . . It does not greatly matter what most people eat or drink because they are not working to the limit of their capacity either in quality or quantity. To the few who are working on the finest edge of their utmost powers it matters a great deal. You can be a Sancho Panza on any food provided there is enough of it. If you want to be a Pythagoras, you have to be more careful.

George Bernard Shaw in letter to
Thomas Demetrius O'Bolger, 1920

The last chapter was concerned mainly with specific diseases associated with meat and animal products, with clinical and field findings involving groups of people in health and sickness, and with the painfully slow willingness of orthodox medicine to accept the vital importance of correct nutrition. The more positive approach must deal in the main with comparative food values and with tracing a brief outline of the vital interrelationships between certain nutrients – a subject as relevant to flesh-eaters as to frugivores. But the whole question of health and nutrition is so large, extending so far beyond (yet often linked to) the place of animal food in our diet, that it is possible to explore the matter only sketchily in a short book that is attempting to present a more general argument for a non-flesh diet. Further reading is widely available and I mention some of the leading authorities. (See also the Bibliography on page 186.)

However, those qualified often disagree most and some of the statements made by people who detest or distrust the idea of adopting a more humane diet are a good deal sillier than the silliest of its supporters. The latter have, on the whole, to be more careful than the former if for no other reason than that they are more vulnerable in a predominantly meat-eating society. Many people must have been deterred from giving up meat by the sometimes pathetically foolish advice given on diet in some of the popular 'authorities'. In one of the best-known of these, *Black's Medical Dictionary* (1961), in the section on diet, one reads this ludicrous passage:

> The great objection to vegetarianism . . . lies in the enormous bulk of vegetable food necessary, mainly in consequence of the relatively large amount of water it contains. Thus, if one were to subsist on nothing but lentil porridge, about 5 pounds of it would be necessary daily; or if one lived solely on green vegetables and succulent fruits, the impossible weight of about 30 pounds every day would be necessary to a fairly hard-working healthy man.

Such gems of nonsense leave one momentarily groping for words. One has to discard the false premise and replace it with a factual proposition before one can even begin to communicate. The naïve ploy of the lentil (nowadays a widely and deservedly recommended ingredient of many recipes) makes as much sense as to point out that in order to get enough iron by subsisting on 'nothing but milk', that 'fairly hard-working healthy man' would have to drink 8,000 fluid ounces every day. Just who would consider subsisting on 5 pounds of lentil porridge (a dish, I may say, I have never even come across) is not suggested, though it would certainly be someone far nuttier than any vegetarian one is likely to encounter. Only a strangely ignorant or prejudiced critic could suggest that flesh abstainers would expect to function adequately on so limited a range of primate food. He can certainly never have asked himself what the water content of *meat* happens to be – the percentage in lean, grilled steak is, as it happens, 59 per cent and the toxic wastes from the animal's bloodstream, plus the bacteria from putrefaction and often diseased tissue, make it very dirty water indeed – for all that the grilling should destroy the bacteria.

After which rather negative skirmishing, it must be stated – and unequivocally so – that neither vegetarians (lacto-) nor vegans eat, nor need to eat, appreciably larger quantities of plant or any other foods than meat-eaters. If anything, their total intake is probably less, for while many vegetarians may tackle larger or more balanced salads than most meat-eaters, and while vegans are likely to eat more nuts and pulses, both classes tend to eat less of the refined, processed and prepared foods to which those for whom greed ranks above need are apt to be addicted. Perhaps the best way to dismiss some of the standard absurdities is to study the tables on pages 91-97, showing the composition of various foods and based on the second edition (1970) of the *Manual of Nutrition*, published by HMSO for the Ministry of Agriculture, Fisheries and Food. The composition is given per 100 grams and reference to this table will use the abbreviation (MN). A column has been added for the percentage of water in each food listed, and this percentage is taken from the comparable tables of the *Nutritive Value of Foods* (text reference (NVF) will be used), prepared by the Consumer and Food Economics Research Division of the Agricultural Research Service of Washington, DC, for the United States Department of Agriculture's 'Home and Garden Bulletin' no. 72 (revised 1970).

Comparison of these two tables shows some contradictions, mostly small. Various factors account for these. Allowance has to be made for experimental errors, for compositional variations between different areas of growth, for freshness, for the extent to which some foods have been dried, and the degree to which others have been cooked; it may or may not be relevant that that notoriously overcooked object the British Brussels sprout rates only 16 kilocalories (calories for short – see page 99) to 100 grams in the (MN) table, whereas (NVF) shows over double this figure at 36. There is a similar discrepancy for boiled cabbage and both vegetables also fail to show anything like as satisfactory a protein content in Britain as in America. These differences – in calories, protein or both – may be seen in other vegetables listed, including peas, potatoes, tomatoes, onions, mushrooms and carrots. (Today's figures for meat are moving towards leaner compositions, and with more fat trimmed away.)

Certain plant foods of importance are inadequately covered or not listed in (MN) at all and the following values from (NVF) should be useful for considering alongside the (MN) table. However, more recent compilations in the UK take greater account of 'ethnic' and vegetarian/vegan foods. They are available in print and on disc.

(MN) Table

Per 100g

	No.	Food	Water %	Energy value Kcal	Energy value KJ	Protein g	Fat g	Carbohydrate (as monosaccharide) g
Milk	1	Cow's milk, whole, fluid	87	65	272	3.3	3.8	4.8
	2	Cream, single	80	189	792	2.8	18.0	4.2
	3	Yoghurt, natural	88	57	239	3.6	2.6	5.2
Cheese	4	Cheese, cheddar	37	412	1,726	25.4	34.5	0
	5	Cheese, cottage	79	115	482	15.1	4.0	4.5
Meat	6	Bacon, average	8	476	1,994	11.0	48.0	0
	7	Beef, average	50	313	1,311	14.8	28.2	0
	8	Beef, stewed steak	59	242	1,014	29.0	14.0	0
	9	Chicken, roast	58	184	771	29.6	7.3	0
	10	Lamb, roast	58	284	1,190	25.0	20.4	0
	11	Pork, average	50	408	1,710	12.0	40.0	0
Fish	12	Cod, haddock, white fish	66	69	289	16.0	0.5	0
	13	Sardines, canned in oil	62	285	1,194	20.4	22.6	0
Eggs	14	Eggs, fresh	74	158	662	11.9	12.3	0
Fats	15	Butter	15	745	3,122	0.5	82.5	0
	16	Lard, dripping	0	894	3,746	0	99.3	0
	17	Margarine	16	769	3,222	0.2	85.3	0

	No.	Food	Water %	Energy value Kcal	Energy value KJ	Protein g	Fat g	Carbohydrate (as monosaccharide) g
	18	Oils (vegetable), salad and cooking	0	899	3,767	0	99.9	0
Vegetables	19	Beans, canned in tomato sauce	71	92	385	6.0	0.4	17.3
	20	Beans, broad	90	69	289	7.2	0.5	9.5
	21	Beetroot, boiled	91	44	184	1.8	0	9.9
	22	Brussels sprouts, boiled	88	16	67	2.4	0	1.7
	23	Cabbage, raw	92	28	117	1.5	0	5.8
	24	Cabbage, boiled	94	8	34	0.8	0	1.3
	25	Carrots, old, cooked	91	23	96	0.7	0	5.4
	26	Cauliflower	93	24	101	3.4	0	2.8
	27	Parsnips	82	49	205	1.7	0	11.3
	28	Peas, fresh or quick frozen, boiled	82	49	205	5.0	0	7.7
	29	Potatoes, boiled	80	79	331	1.4	0	19.7
	30	Spinach	92	21	88	2.7	0	2.8
	31	Sweetcorn, tinned	81	95	398	2.6	0.8	20.5
Fruit	32	Apples	85	46	193	0.3	0	12.0
	33	Apricots, dried	25	182	768	4.8	0	43.4
	34	Bananas	76	76	318	1.1	0	19.2
	35	Dates	22	248	1,039	2.0	0	63.9
	36	Figs, dried	23	213	892	3.6	0	52.9
	37	Grapefruit	89	22	92	0.6	0	5.3

Per 100g

No.	Food	Water %	Energy value Kcal	KJ	Protein g	Fat g	Carbohydrate (as monosaccharide) g
38	*Oranges*	86	35	147	0.8	0	8.5
39	*Pears*	83	41	172	0.3	0	10.6
40	*Sultanas*	18	249	1,043	1.7	0	64.7
Nuts							
41	*Almonds*	5	580	2,430	20.5	53.5	4.3
42	*Coconut, dessicated*	51(c)	608	2,548	6.6	62.0	6.4
43	*Peanuts, roasted*	2	586	2,455	28.1	49.0	8.6
44	*Barley, pearl, dry*	11	360	1,508	7.7	1.7	83.6
45	*Bread, white, enriched*	36	253	1,060	8.3	1.7	54.6
Cereals							
46	*Bread, wholemeal*	36	241	1,010	9.6	3.1	46.7
47	*Oatmeal*	3	400	1,676	12.1	8.7	72.8
48	*Spaghetti*	68	364	1,525	9.9	1.0	84.0
Preserves							
49	*Honey*	17	288	1,207	0.4	0	76.4
50	*Sugar, white*	Trace	394	1,651	0	0	105.5

Composition per ounce of a few basic foods for comparison with the fuller tables based on grams (pages 91–93)

	Carbs g	Energy value (cals/kJ)	Protein g	Calcium mg	Iron mg	Vit A µg	Vit D mg	Vit C mg	Fat g
Dates	18.1	70/295	0.69	19	0.5	3	0	0	0
White fish	0	19/82	4.5	7	0.3	0	0	0	0.1
Cheddar cheese	0	117/490	7.2	230	0.2	119	0.10	0	9.8
Bananas	5.5	22/90	0.3	2	0.1	9	0	3	0
Lentils	15.1	84/351	6.8	11	2.2	2	0	0	0
Beef (cooked)	0	69/288	8.2			0	0	0	4.0
Beans (haricot)	12.9	73/305	6.1	51	1.9	0	0	0	0
Eggs	0	45/188	3.4	16	0.7	85	0.43	0	3.5
Oatmeal	20.6	113/475	3.4	16	1.2	0	0	0	2.5
Peanuts (roasted)	2.4	166/697	8.0	17	0.6	0	0	0	13.9

Values for almonds are similar to those for peanuts, but contain 5.8 g of protein and a lot more calcium
Cobnuts have 2.6 g protein (calories 113)
Walnuts have 3.6 g protein
Brazils have 3.9 g protein
Brown bread has 2.5 g protein

(Details taken from the *Manual of Nutrition*, Ministry of Agriculture, HMSO, 1970.)

(NVF) Table

No.	Calcium mg	Iron mg	Vitamin A (retinol equivalents) µg	Thiamine (B₁) mg	Riboflavin (B₂) mg	Nicotinic Acid (B₃) mg	Total Equivalents mg	Ascorbic Acid (C) mg
1	120	0.1	40(av.)	0.04	0.15	0.1	0.9	1(a)
2	100	0.1	155	0.03	0.13	0.1	0.8	1
3	140	0.1	39	0.05	0.19	0.1	0.9	0
4	810	0.6	420	0.04	0.50	0.1	5.2	0
5	80	0.4	27	0.03	0.27	0.1	3.2	0
6	10	1.0	0	0.40	0.15	1.5	4.0	0
7	10	4.0	0	0.07	0.20	5.0	7.8	0
8	8	5.0	0	0.05	0.22	5.0	10.4	0
9	15	2.6	0	0.04	0.14	4.9	10.0	0
10	4	4.3	0	0.10	0.25	4.5	9.8	0
11	10	1.0	0	1.00	0.20	5.0	7.7	0
12	25	1.0	0	0.06	0.10	3.0	6.0	0
13	409	4.0	30	0	0.20	5.0	8.6	0
14	56	2.5	300	0.10	0.35	0.1	3.0	0
15	15	0.2	995	0	0	0	0	0
16	0	0	0	0	0	0	0	0
17	4	0.3	900	0	0	0	0.1	0

No.	Calcium	Iron	Vitamin A (retinol equivalents)	Thiamine (B₁)	Riboflavin (B₂)	Nicotinic Acid (B₃)	Total Equivalents	Ascorbic Acid (C)
	mg	mg	µg	mg	mg	mg	mg	mg
18	0	0	0	0	0	0.	0	0
19	62	2.1	50	0.06	0.04	0.5	1.5	3
20	30	1.1	22	0.28	0.05	4.0	5.0	30
21	30	0.7	0	0.02	0.04	0.1	0.4	5
22	27	0.6	67	0.06	0.10	0.4	0.9	35
23	65	1.0	50	0.06	0.05	0.2	0.5	60
24	58	0.5	50	0.03	0.03	0.2	0.3	20
25	48	0.6	2,000	0.06	0.05	0.6	0.7	6
26	18	0.6	5	0.10	0.10	0.6	1.4	70
27	55,	0.6	0	0.10	0.09	1.0	1.3	15
28	13	1.2	50	0.25	0.11	1.5	2.3	15
29	4	0.5	0	0.08	0.03	0.8	1.2	4-15(b)
30	70	3.2	1,000	0.12	0.20	0.6	1.2	60
31	5	0.5	35	0.03	0.05	0.9	0.3	4
32	4	0.3	5	0.04	0.02	0.1	0.1	5
33	92	4.1	600	0	0.20	3.0	3.4	0
34	7	0.4	33	0.04	0.07	0.6	0.8	10
35	68	1.6	10	0.07	0.04	2.0	2.3	0
36	284	4.2	8	0.10	0.13	1.7	2.2	0
37	17	0.3	0	0.05	0.02	0.2	0.3	40

No.	Calcium	Iron	Vitamin A (retinol equivalents)	Thiamine (B₁)	Riboflavin (B₂)	Nicotinic Acid (B₃)		Ascorbic Acid (C)
						Total	Equivalents	
	mg	mg	µg	mg	mg	mg	mg	mg
38	41	0.3	8	0.10	0.03	0.2	0.3	50
39	8	0.2	2	0.03	0.03	0.2	0.3	3
40	52	1.8	0	0.10	0.30	0.5	0.6	0
41	247	4.2	0	0.32	0.25	2.0	4.9	0
42	22	3.6	0	0.06	0.04	0.6	1.8	0
43	61	2.0	0	0.23	0.10	16.0	20.8	0
44	10	0.7	0	0.12	0.08	2.5	2.2	0
45	100	1.8	0	0.18	0.02	1.4	2.3	0
46	28	3.0	0	0.24	0.09	2.6	1.9	0
47	55	4.1	0	0.50	0.10	1.0	2.8	0
48	23	1.2	0	0.09	0.06	1.7	1.8	0
49	5	0.4	0	0	0.05	0.2	0.2	0
50	1	0	0	0	0	0	0	0

Key: (a) less than 1 mg (b) vitamin C falls during storage (c) grated, fresh

Avocado A 240-gram Californian winter avocado can afford 370 calories, and 5 grams of protein. Also 37 grams of fat and useful amounts of calcium, vitamin A, the vitamin B complex, etc.

Dried peas, beans and nuts These most valuable foods are hardly given attention by (MN), though dry lentils are admitted to contain 295 calories per 100 grams, with protein at 23.8 g and good amounts of calcium and iron. Split dried peas showing over 1 calorie per gram weight and 20 g of protein per cup of 250 g, should surely have been included, as should butter, haricot and other dried beans whose energy value and protein content are quantitatively and qualitatively excellent. It is equally regrettable that only three kinds of nuts are shown. The most important exclusions are: cashews – in their popular roasted form a cup of 140 g produces 785 calories, 24 g protein (unroasted 20 g), 64 g fat, 53 milligrams calcium, and other significant nutrients; pecans – better known in the USA than in the UK, these excellent nuts hold 740 calories to 108 g, also 10 g protein, 77 g fat, 79 mg calcium, etc.; and walnuts, which come out at 790 calories per 126 g, 26 g protein, 75 g fat, 380 mg vitamin A.

Rice Brown (unpolished) rice gives over 1 calorie per gram weight when cooked and over 2.5 g protein per 100 g, but it has less value when taken in its white and enriched form. Much is 'lost' by absorption of water in cooking, there being 12 g protein to 185 g raw weight.

Soya beans Dried soya beans, cooked, produce well over 1 calorie per gram, also 10 per cent protein, 5 g fat and much higher amounts of calcium, iron, etc., than does meat. A significant comparison may be made between a cup (100 g) of dried nonfat cow's milk, giving 360 calories, 35 g protein, and 1 g fat, and a cup (100 g) of low-fat, dried soya bean powder showing 250 calories, 52 g protein, 5.6 g fat.[1] Soya bean flour should also be compared with enriched white flour, 120 g of the former producing 425 calories, 52 g protein, 8 g fat, 315 mg calcium, 10.9 mg iron and 96 international units of vitamin A, against 115 g of the latter showing only 12 g protein, 1 g fat, 18 mg calcium, 3.3 mg iron and no vitamin A for the same amount of calories.

Wheat germ Raw wheat germ has 363 calories per 100 g, 27 g protein, 11 g fat, 72 mg calcium, 9.4 mg iron and important mineral quantities. A very cheap source of protein.

Yeast A tablespoon (8 g) of dry yeast yields roughly 25 calories, 3 g protein and high proportions of essential minerals and vitamins. Of great importance in food technology, not only for bread and alcoholic beverages, yeast – like wheat germ, bran and the cereals – is at last receiving serious attention from nutritionists and the medical world.

There are many other food sources that contribute to a balanced and healthy diet based on plant rather than animal life, some of them foreign to the conventional British nutritionist, yet important enough to be listed in the (NVF) tables. Dandelion greens, for instance. Cooked, 180 g of this remarkable vegetable ('weed' is an insult) give 60 calories, 4 g protein, 252 mg calcium and 21,060 international units of vitamin A, which puts dandelions into the top league with liver for vitamin A and above even carrots, spinach and dried apricots. It would also not be irrelevant to mention that brown (Barbados) sugar compares well with white, which is valueless except for calories. The brown at least holds 187 mg of calcium (much of it the residue from a chemical used in the process known in the trade as defecation!), 7.5 mg iron and small amounts of vitamins per cup of 220 g, supplying a more moderate 280 calories against white sugar's 770 (NVF); but we are doubtless better without either. This sort of reflection, however, threatens to lead into the more general area of health foods, already well covered in nutritional texts.

Before we examine individually the main nutrients listed in the (MN) table , we might consider the question of calories. Calories are not nutrients, but units of heat used in expressing the energy content of foods. They come in two sizes, small and large. The smaller calorie is the amount of heat needed to raise the temperature of a gram of water by one degree centigrade. This doesn't add up to very much, so the large calorie (or kilocalorie) is usually referred to for nutritional purposes (see Symbols and conversion factors, page 6).

As the (NVF) table shows (and comparison may be made with the tables on pages 91-97), a pound (453.6 grams) of grilled, lean sirloin beefsteak is needed to supply 920 calories. Take lean and fat and you have a figure of 1,760. These are not sensational figures if it is calories you are after, when one sees that walnuts will provide some 2,700 calories for the same weight, and almonds, cashews and brazils much the same. Hazelnuts top 3,000 calories to the pound. Those who believe it does something for their masculine image to boast of putting away a pound of steak at a sitting would have more to brag about if they had managed to get round a pound of peanuts. According to the National

Academy of Sciences' list of recommended dietary allowances, whose statistics were not intended for Peruvian peasants, they would have consumed enough calories to keep a full-grown American male on the go for a whole day, having swallowed 300 grams of fat, enough protein for two days, and over 800 grams of carbohydrates. A pound of pecans would give them even more calories and fat, but a saner quantity of protein and some 600 i.u. of vitamin A against the paltry 80 offered in a pound of lean sirloin. Other and more serious comparisons could be made, all pointing to the indisputable superiority, in a balanced diet, of nuts over animal flesh.

The fact of the matter is that nuts are an excellent source of nutrition and one that has been almost totally disregarded in a society determined to centre its eating on meat rather than on the foods for which our species is specifically constructed and chemically attuned. Nuts more than almost any other made-for-man as distinct from man-made food put the 5-pounds-of-lentil-porridge school to flight, their high nutritive value making it unnecessary that they be eaten in such large quanties as the watery meats.

Beans and pulses, hardly less neglected in the West until recently, also help greatly to achieve an easier and more natural balance of nutrients, reducing the total food intake with all the extra mental and physical alertness this invariably brings. Whatever way one cuts the cake, the answer remains the same – there is no valid reason for claiming superiority for meat over a vegetarian diet. Even if dairy products are excluded, plant foods can and should supply our species with everything that it needs. As nutritionists such as Dr Frey Ellis and Professor J. W. T. Dickerson have made abundantly clear, plant foods are not only absurdly undervalued for their nutritional worth, but if fed directly to man rather than after processing through animals they can increase the nutritive yield per acre by up to ten fold. Soya beans, for example, yield seven times as much amino acid per acre as milk production and eight times as much as egg production. An animal must consume seven plant calories in order to produce one calorie's worth of human food . . .

The only reservation one must make about the completeness and adequacy of a fleshless diet, apart from the question of sufficient vitamin B_{12} for strict vegans under civilized conditions (see Chapter 7), is that freshness of food is always important, whether it is of plant or animal origin, and allowance must be made for this when comparing the needs of urban man with the requirements of those fortunate enough to have access to food at the point of growth and time of harvest.

Protein

More popular myths have been built around food than around almost any other aspect of our daily lives, and probably more nonsense has been talked about protein than any other nutrient. It has received a disproportionate amount of attention and reverence and it therefore takes an undue amount of space to redress the balance.

For many years proteins were misleadingly classified as either 'first class' or 'second class'. The 'first class' proteins were identified as being in the animal foods (meat, eggs and dairy products), while the 'second class' were those found in plant life. Having helped to vilify and misrepresent the argument for a more natural and healthful eating pattern, the 'first and second class' classification has at last been abandoned. In its place there is now a concern to establish how useful a particular protein is to the body, and to express its 'utilization' on a numerical scale.

Nutritionally proteins are assessed according to the amount of each essential amino acid they contain, and that amino acid which falls furthest below the standard of reference protein is said to be the limiting amino for the protein in question. For instance, the limiting amino acid in wheat and millet is lysine and that in beans is methionine. If the diet contains both wheat (e.g., in bread) and beans, and provided enough of these are taken at the same meal, the protein requirement will have been satisfied, a better quality protein meal having been obtained than from either eaten by itself. From a nutritional point of view animal or vegetable protein should not be differentiated. A protein that contains all the essential amino acids in suitable proportions has a high biological value and so is a high quality or 'complete' protein. Meat, dairy products, whole wheat, most beans and other plant forms, are complete proteins in this sense, but the only single-food truly complete proteins are in human milk and hens' eggs.

This new method of assessment, however, is still slanted by some in favour of animal foods (though no longer by the suggestion, now seen as untenable, that plant foods are inadequate), in that eggs may be chosen as the ideal reference protein. An odd choice at a time when there is wide doubt of the wisdom of including eggs at all in the adequate human diet, especially for men, in view of their high cholesterol level (*Mind and Body*, page 1030, vol. 3, Orbis, 1971).

If one accepts this point of reference it gives values in the 60-80 range for animal proteins and a figure of mostly under 50 for plant proteins, but the point to note is that the values are now based on the *proportions* of essential and non-essential amino acids and no longer on the misleading basis of 'first' or 'second' class.[2] The ten essential amino acids are threonine, valine, methionine, isoleucine, leucine, phenylalanine, tryptophan, lysine and (in childhood) histidine and arginine, and these have to be supplied in our food. Our bodies are able to manufacture the non-essential acids. As proteins are now judged on their individual merits instead of being lumped together, if one plant protein that is short of essential amino acid 'A', but has plenty of 'B' and enough of the others, is added to another that has adequate 'A' but less of 'B', together they make a total protein meal that is just as good as one of the 'first class' proteins.

This principle of mixing complementary plant proteins is employed to create nutritious and inexpensive protein foods for undeveloped countries and it also explains why a normal vegetarian diet supplies enough nourishment. The supplementary value (the *mixture*) of cereals and nuts is why the now popular *muesli* breakfast foods are so extraordinarily sustaining for the small amount that is needed. This more realistic and certainly more scientific method of valuing proteins has done much to bring greater recognition of the importance of plant foods. It has strengthened our realization, so long buried by the prejudice of habit and its concomitant influence on both professional and lay opinion, that man does not need to eat any animal products whatsoever; so long, that is, as what is eaten is reasonably balanced and wholesome.

The new method of evaluating proteins has also enabled us to consider certain forms of food, long hallowed by greed and such irrelevancies as status-symbolism, on their own merits. Consider, for instance, that status-symbol of our time, so often quoted as a supreme source of nutrition and for so long hard-sold by the massive American meat industry, the sacred beefsteak – about as high as you can go in flesh foods if it is protein you are after. As the tables on pages 91-97 show, 100 grams (3½ ounces) of stewing steak has a protein content of about 29 per cent, but it also yields 14 grams of deeply suspect, high-cholesterol fat (and much more than 14 grams if you go for non-lean meat), up to 15 grams of saturated fatty acids, 59 per cent of dirty water, 242 calories, 5.0 mg of iron, 5.0 mg of vitamin B_3, some other B vitamins and negligible amounts of anything else worth having. Compare these figures with those for almonds, providing only about 5 per cent of water, 580 calories, a better quality protein, more but healthier fat, far less saturated fatty acids and a much greater weight of the unsaturated. Almonds also give significantly larger quantities of iron, etc., and a soaring (even unnecessary) 247 mg of calcium against steak's eight.

Other and equally 'orthodox' authorities have shown a different approach to the relative nutritional merits of basic foods, but the inconsistencies are minor and almost always tending towards rather than away from the more balanced view this book is attempting to present. As an instance, in its section on protein *Mind and Body* (Part 95, Orbis, 1972), apparently taking into account water content, shows thirteen sources of protein, giving a value of 10 to dried skimmed milk and moving down the scale to show sunflower seeds and peanuts at 8 apiece; Cheddar cheese at 7.25; dried milk, green peas and haricot beans at 7; almonds at 6; beef at 4.80; evaporated milk at 2; fresh green peas at 1.60; and liquid milk at less than 1. Were the value of soya and wheat germ also acknowledged, they would top the list with ease.

In the protein stakes it is easy to see why the soya bean has been described as the most valued plant on earth. With its up-to-23 per cent of fat, not to mention vitamins A, B_1 and B_2, many vital trace elements, iron, calcium, phosphorus, a high calorie count, little or no starch, low carbohydrate content and a rich source of the essential amino acid lysine (the main lack in bread, which otherwise can be a good source of balanced nutrients), there is little wonder that food technologists are giving it so much attention. Filling without fattening, it could be the answer not merely to a maiden's prayer, but also and more importantly to the needs of those two-thirds of the world's population known to be undernourished. Its slight deficiency in the amino acid methionine can be overcome by blending it with other plant proteins, as already indicated, and fortifying it with cereal proteins will also increase the biological value to acceptable levels. Such supplementation is of course necessary with all foods, and no less so with meat. The amino acid minimum for adults, incidentally, can be obtained from a pint of soya bean milk or cow's milk and about four slices of bread each day. Remember that soya flour contains all its nutrients in a far more concentrated form than does the bean.

The soya bean's main use at present is as meal for high-protein food for livestock and for adding to the protein content in various products for human consumption, but as mentioned in Chapter 2 its role in the shape of meat analogues and other forms of protein for human consumption is increasing steadily as its value as a direct food for man is being recognized.[3]

It may surprise some readers to know that leaves are a further excellent source of protein. 'The nutritional value of leaf protein,' announced *The Lancet* (24 August, 1968) '– better than most seed proteins and as good as many animal proteins – has been known for many years', and in his paper 'Protein Metabolism' (*Proceedings of the Royal Society of Medicine*, vol. 60, November, 1967) Dr N. W. Pirie described how leaves, containing 15-25 per cent protein of good biological value, have been processed on a large scale at Rothamstead Experimental Station. The ideal leaf-source is a by-product from some other crop, such as banana, jute, ramie, sugar beet, sugar cane, sweet potato or peas and beans harvested for canning or freezing. Such sources are at present largely wasted. 'Once the idea of using leaf protein as a human food is accepted it would, however, be reasonable to grow crops specially for this purpose because a greater yield of protein would be got from an acre in a year in this way than by conventional agriculture.' In a later paper, 'The Present Position of Research on the Use of Leaf Protein as a Human Food', Dr Pirie stated: 'Equipment has been designed with which 60-70 per cent of the protein can be extracted from various leafy crops . . . The product contains . . . 20-30 per cent of highly unsaturated fat. Human and animal feeding experiments show that it is better than other plant proteins.' (*Plant Foods for Human Nutrition*, vol. 1, no. 4, November, 1969.)

In case it is suspected that food value calculations are being slanted by anxious governments in favour of plant foods because of the recent realization of the inevitability of population pressure and world re-sources compelling a reduction in stock farming, it may be of interest to note what an even older authority has had to say. The Medical Research Council's *Nutritive Values of Wartime Food* (HMSO) made it equally apparent that a mixed vegetarian diet will supply all the nutritive essentials. Their figures showed 16 per cent for sirloin, 14 per cent for steak, 17 per cent for stewing steak, 18 per cent for carcass veal and 25 per cent for corned beef. In this table fish boasts as high a protein content as sirloin, with cod, sole, salmon, crab and kipper at 16, 16, 17, 20 and 19 per cent respectively. Fresh eggs rate only 12.5 per cent, though the dried egg of wartime beat all rivals listed at 45.8 per cent, yeast food at 43.1 per cent being a close runner-up. Contrary to popular belief, fish and eggs do not make large contributions to most nutrients, though they are useful sources of vitamin D, and both furnish vitamin B_{12}. Fish is now applauded for its content of polyunsaturated fats.

Unsurprisingly (at least to the higher primates and vegetarian man), then as now it was acknowledged that it is the nuts and pulses that present the greatest challenge to the over-stated claims for the virtues of animal foods – though the wider use and availability of cereal crops keep the grain foods highest of all plant protein sources at the present time. Haricots at 21.4 per cent, lentils at 23.8 per cent (some at 29 per cent), dried peas at 24.5 per cent, almonds at 20.5 per cent, peanuts at 28.1 per cent, soya at 40.4 per cent – even thirty years ago these percentages allowed no justification for the traditional belief in the superiority of flesh foods.

What is more important than the reduced significance of meat is this now more widely acknowledged value of the plant alternatives. In his paper 'Proteins', Dr F. Wokes has written:

> Although animal foods are generally considered to be richer sources of protein, various plant foods such as nuts and pulses have a higher protein content than meat, milk or eggs calculated either on their composition as prepared for cooking or eating, or on the calorie basis. Deficiency of some essential amino acids such as lysine or methionine in individual plant proteins can be largely overcome by blending different plant proteins producing mixtures with biological values perhaps 15-25 per cent below those of human milk protein. (*Plant Foods for Human Nutrition*, vol. 1, no. 1, May, 1968.)

Great Britain even more than America has lagged way behind the rest of the world in appreciating the range, uses and food value of nuts and the pulses. On the continent of Europe, particularly in Greece and in India and most Asian countries, their nutritive value is well known and utilized. They are one of the most economical and accessible forms of protein. Little used in the UK except when tinned and covered in tomato sauce, the haricot bean has many uses, as has the valuable and similarly neglected butter bean. But delicatessens, health food shops and lately even supermarkets can usually offer such changes – well-known already in the USA – as the red kidney, borlotti, adzuki, gram, dhal, cannellini, black-eyed and ceci beans. Beans, in short, greatly widen the culinary horizons of anyone wishing to subsist pleasurably on plant foods. The appreciable quantities and quality of protein in the common pulses, together with other foods, supply the range of amino acids necessary for health.[4] Sprouted dried beans, the shoots being delicious, are another valuable source of nourishment. But it cannot be overemphasized that, taken all in all, the most overlooked and valuable source of protein and most of the other nutrients essential to man is the nut. Highly nutritious, its value has quite simply been neglected in favour of meat products for the richer countries and cereals for the poorer. In an address to the Northern Nut Growers' Association at Stamford, Connecticut, as far back as 1917, Dr John Harvey Kellog pointed out that one pound of walnut meat has the equivalent food value of four pounds of red meat or ten pounds of boiling chicken or 7¾ pints of milk or 22 pounds of lobster. For sheer food value, a 126 g cup of walnuts producing 790 calories and 26 g protein may be compared with 8 fl oz of cow's milk producing 160 calories and 9 g protein (NVF). An acre of walnuts will supply more than 1,000 pounds of shelled meats with a food value of 3,000,000 calories. This is twenty times the amount that the same acre would yield in beef. The protein quantity of the nuts would be as great as beef and of superior quality. It is to man's shame that these values in nuts and the pulses have been ignored for so long by those whose eating pattern has been under the thumb of the powerful meat industry and Western man's acquired preference for animal flesh. Here, as Kellog said, '. . . is a veritable treasure of wealth, a potential food supply which may save the world from any suggestion of hunger for centuries to come if properly utilized . . . The nut should no longer be considered a table luxury. It should become a staple article of food and may most profitably replace the pork and meats of various sorts which are inferior foods and recognized as prolific sources of disease.'[5]

His words are even more applicable today than they were in 1917, but as Professor Henry Bailey Stevens has pointed out, the inertia against change has been tremendous. Producers trained in the skills of their commodity and involved with heavy capital investments, look for more of their own kind of business, not for less or for diversification. Commodity organizations intensify such a viewpoint and can turn definite pressures against changes in the status quo. Processors, distributors and financial interests reflect a similar attitude. The most likely factors to bring about the change-over are the soaring cost of animal products and a hungry world demanding that the affluent nations should recognize the ecological priority of a generally accepted (and, as it happens, more humane) diet.

Should I seem to have strayed a little from the point, these asides relate as much to protein as to any other constituent. No vegan should lack protein in view of the high concentrations in nuts, soya beans, cereals, whole grains, dried peas and beans, brewers' yeast, sunflower seeds, sesame seeds, wheat germ, avocados and plant milk; and the lacto-vegetarian's acceptance of cow's milk, cheese and eggs on top of all the other protein sources available to him increases the absurdity of any suggestion that a diet merely excluding actual flesh could be in any way inadequate.

As is widely acknowledged, it is all too easy in the West to eat too much rather than too little. If we eat something of poor protein content but high calorific value, we may well be absorbing more calories than we need without obtaining enough protein. Hence the importance of understanding the balances involved – whether one eats meat or not. However, the danger is not great and in the developed countries most of us eat more than we need.[6]

This section might best be rounded off by considering just what protein is in fact obtained from a modest vegan or lacto-vegetarian diet for a single day. Calories must be taken into account at the same time because of their inter-relationship. The following is not being suggested as a necessarily perfect or exciting menu, but as an example of a very simple meal pattern for one day only. The first of the two columns of figures on the right represents grams of protein, the second column calories. Authorities differ slightly in their recommended daily dietary allowance of proteins and calories, but for the purposes of this sample we can take the needs of a grown man aged 22-35 as being roughly 2,800 calories and 65 g protein. Some authorities have suggested a protein intake of 1 g per kg body-weight (hence 70 g protein for the 'average' (?) man of 70 kg), but today it is considered that less than this is enough, provided some of the protein is of high quality. Proteins provide materials for growth and repair of body tissues, but in well-balanced diets do not furnish energy. In excess, they slow down the physical and mental processes.

Breakfast:	2 slices wholemeal bread	6 :	120
	½ oz nut butter	4 :	90
Lunch:	4 oz potatoes	5 :	105
	3 oz green beans, etc.	4 :	60
	3 oz Cheddar cheese *or* almonds	21 :	445
	Orange, banana, pear	3 :	265
Dinner:	½ lettuce	2 :	30
	1 tomato	2 :	40
	2 oz dried dates	5 :	160
	2 slices rye or pumpernickel bread	4 :	60
	½ oz cashew nut cream	3 :	60

2 oz cheese *or* nuts	14 : 30
	71 : 1,665

Not exactly a gourmand's idea of high living, yet giving more protein than is needed by a healthy, adult male. Such figures are difficult to relate to the popular concept of vegetarians as protein-deficient. The opposite seems to be the case. What is needed, in view of the fact that this day's menu in fact omits a number of items that would normally be added (plant or cow's milk, beans, yoghurt, eggs, additional salad vegetables, fruit juices, macaroni, rice, salad or cooking oils, beverages, perhaps the odd soup or apple pie), is some way of *reducing* the protein. The calories are obviously going to look after themselves. This reduction could be achieved by using butter or margarine instead of nut-based butters or cream. Where peanut butter supplies 4 g protein to the half-ounce, butter or margarine give only 1 g to 2 ounces. Alternatively, 2 ounces of cheese or nuts in place of 3 ounces would take off 7 g of protein. The ease with which the protein intake can be overdone is shown by the value of a cup of lentils – 20 g (twice as many as a cup of milk) – though admittedly a cup of cooked lentils is a fairly demanding way of getting nourishment that can more easily be obtained from other plant sources, as *Black's Medical Dictionary* obviously knew. Even an ounce of wheat germ sprinkled over an ounce of cornflakes at breakfast will supply a further 9 g of protein, never mind the milk. Add an egg to the breakfast menu, as the lacto-vegetarian may wish to do, and a further 6 g of protein has been provided.

It can be seen, therefore, that those who eat a high proportion of meat and little else can more easily fall below the target of 2,800 calories. To get this number would mean eating over 3 pounds of lean steak every day, which would be far less beneficial than achieving the same calorie count by eating nearly a pound of walnuts – though neither is recommended. Far better to step up the calorie intake, although few of us lack carbohydrates unless our diets are hopelessly inadequate or unbalanced; if the calories are adequate, protein needs will be satisfied.

Carbohydrates

Where proteins are primarily useful to build the body and repair the tissues, carbohydrates are sources of dietary fibre and provide us with the heat and energy we need to function each day. They have provided a large part of the calorie count of our diet ever since cereals became of major importance. The principal sources are best found in whole grain cereals, breads, cornmeal, potatoes, macaroni products, dried beans and roasted nuts. Unfortunately all too many of us instead of recognizing the value of such sources as barley, rye, buckwheat and brown rice, get a lot of our carbohydrates from such substances as sugar and its many products and from those cakes, biscuits and so forth which are usually made from refined flours and have rightly been condemned by all nutritionists. Writers of the calibre of Doris Grant and John Yudkin have said most of what needs to be said on this subject and it is beyond my brief to go into too many details, but it is the starchy staple foods such as bread and potatoes that supply us with many important vitamins, minerals and substantial amounts of protein as well, and these tend to be blamed too readily for obesity. It is true that fat is laid down in the body if more starch food is eaten than is necessary for the energy expended, and it is also true that refining of grains and their products is partly responsible for obesity (because the bran and other nutrients that help the digestion and use of starch are removed), but obesity is brought about chiefly by the total intake of calories being more than we need. As many diets still consist of about 40 per cent fat (an excessive amount in the view of most authorities – gram for gram, fats furnish over twice as many calories as do carbohydrates), 12 per cent protein and less than 50 per cent carbohydrate (against a carbohydrate intake of up to 80 per cent starch in some less developed countries), quite clearly the omnivorous 'fatties' in our midst would be hard put to suggest that starches alone have expanded their waistlines. No dietary standard for carbohydrates has in fact been properly established, as the body can get along very well with far less than most of us take in. Perhaps the most unnecessary source of all is white sugar, which is 100 per cent carbohydrate and robs the body of calcium in the process of being converted into heat. 'Eat less and exercise more' is for most of us the best answer to any anxiety about carbohydrates' place in our lives. As J. W. Lucas of the Radiation Protection Service, Manchester University Institute of Science and Technology, has said, most foods contain a number of energy sources although one particular source may predominate; the energy value of a foodstuff can be calculated if its composition has been determined, and some examples are on the following page.

Fats

Fats also produce heat and energy, offering in addition protection from injury to the kidneys and other organs, and they store long-term energy in various parts of our bodies.

The preferable sources of fat include such vegetable oils as sunflower, soya bean, corn, peanut, cottonseed and olive; nuts, avocados, margarine and various seeds; and eggs and dairy products for those not wishing to exclude animal sources.

The dangers inherent in animal fats, so high in saturated fatty acids, have been discussed exhaustively. As most of us know, the discussion usually centres on the role of saturated versus unsaturated fats. There is no question but that animal fats (including dairy products and eggs) contain cholesterol and it is now generally accepted that an excess constitutes a danger to human health. Vegetable fats, on the other hand, consist mainly of what are called polyunsaturated fats and contain no cholesterol. Instead the substances known as sitosterols are found and these do not behave in the same way. Apart from containing unsaturated fatty acids, vegetable fats are more digestible than animal fats. However, hard margarines, coconut fat, and hydrogenated oils and fats are rich in saturates and best avoided.

Portions of some common foods equivalent to 100 calories (Sherman and Lanford, 1966)

Food	*Approximate portion (oz)*
Butter or margarine	½
Peanut butter	⅗ (tablespoon)
Cheese	⅘ (1 in cube)
Sugar	1
Dry cereal flour	1
Prunes, dry, whole	1⅓
Bread	1⅓ (1⅔ average slice)
Peas (shelled)	3½
Milk	5 (⅔ glass)
Banana	5 (1 medium)
Potato	5 (1 average)
Apple	6 (1 large)
Lean meat	2 (uncooked)
Lettuce	20

As a consequence, it is the belief of vegetarians and many nutritionists and medical people that we do best to use those fats which come from non-animal sources, but with the proviso that the greatest harm from both saturated and unsaturated fats comes when they are used as shortening or cooking oil – that is to say, when heated with other foods, in particular the starches. Almost no one today would defend, in an otherwise adequate diet, the consumption of cakes, pastries, fried bread or potatoes, pie crusts and the like, tempted though most of us are likely to be by such beguiling substances.

The Government's 'Look After Your Heart' campaign recommends, as a first objective, reducing the 'fat calories' in the diet to 35 per cent, but nutritionists have suggested that a fat consumption providing some 25 per cent to 30 per cent of the total calories may be compatible with good health. For those with a penchant for the often depressing evidence of statistics, the following list may be useful (Watts, B. K. and Merrill, A. L., *Composition of Foods*, US Department of Agriculture, 1963):

Saturated and unsaturated fatty acids in foods per 100 grams (edible portion)

Food	Total grams saturated fatty acids	Total grams unsaturated fatty acids
Beef	12	12
Lamb	12	9
Pork	19	27
Cow's milk	15	10
Soya bean milk	3	15
Cheese (Cheddar)	18	12
(cream)	21	13
(cottage)	2	1
Chicken	2	3
Eggs (chickens')	4	6
Herring	2	2
Butter	46	29
Lard	38	56
Corn oil	10	81
Soya bean oil	15	72
Safflower oil	8	87
Shortening (animal and vegetable)	43	52

Food	Total grams saturated fatty acids	Total grams unsaturated fatty acids
Shortening (vegetable)	23	72
Margarine	18-19	60-61
Olive oil	11	83
Cornmeal, white	Trace	3
Wheatgerm	2	8
Avocado pulp	3	9
Olives	2	16
Sesame seeds (whole)	7	40
Soya beans (dry)	3	13
Almonds	4	47
Brazils	13	49
Coconut	30	2
Cashew	8	35
Peanut	10	34
Pecan	5	59
Walnut (black)	4	49

Minerals

No sensible vegan or lacto-vegetarian diet is likely to lack in minerals, but it is relevant to consider the function and chief non-animal sources of some of these.

Iron Iron helps resistance to disease, red blood-cell formation, the maintenance of a correct metabolism and the supply of oxygen to the blood. It is found in whole seeds (wheat, oats, etc.), raisins, wheat germ, lentils, prunes, dates, apricots, spinach and other green leafy vegetables, dried beans, wholemeal bread, brewers' yeast. For ovo-lacto-vegetarians, eggs are a further source. Milk and cheese contain very little, and butter and cooking fats (animal and plant-derived) none at all. Men and women are said to need 10 and 18 mg respectively each day and it is important to children, especially if they were given ordinary cow's milk when very young.

Sodium Sodium plays a vital role in the body's metabolism and most foods contain it. Anyone who lacks it has gone very wrong somewhere, and four to five grams is the amount required daily by the average adult.

The sodium-potassium ratio is far too high in modern diets, but vegetables and fruits, rich in potassium, help to redress the imbalance.

Calcium Building bones and teeth, helping the blood to clot and performing other useful functions that need bother the average vegetarian no more than the average omnivore, calcium accounts for around 1 kg of the human adult's body-weight. Some 800 mg are needed daily. Meat and eggs are a poor source and, though cow's milk has 118 mg to 100 g, a higher figure is obtained from almonds (234), turnip greens (246) and other green vegetables. Cereal foods are a further useful source. Calcium is particularly important for children, women in pregnancy and lactation and at the menopause.

Phosphorus Comprising some 1 per cent of our total body-weight, phosphorus helps the kidneys, the bones and all living and growing tissue. Deficiency is rare, phosphorus being found in all natural food. Vitamin D deficiency can prompt defects of phosphate metabolism, as can kidney disorders and other factors. Toasted wholemeal bread and cashew nuts are good sources, as is the ubiquitous soya bean (cooked), peanuts, cheese and to a lesser extent, eggs. Nuts, beans, leaf and root vegetables, dried fruit – these are all good sources. The Food and Nutrition Board of the American National Research Council recommends that phosphorus intake should be at least equal to that of calcium during childhood and the latter part of pregnancy and lactation. For the rest of the time we shouldn't need to give it a second thought.

Iodine Again no problem. Fish are the main source, of course, but vegetables lead the rest of the field with 28.0 (average) micrograms to 100 g against eggs' 14.5, dairy products' 13.9 and bread and cereals' 10.5. We need about one microgram per kilogram of body-weight and any reasonable diet gives us plenty. Unsurprisingly, seaweed is a good source, also of many other minerals and trace elements including calcium, sodium, iron, copper, potash, phosphate, chlorine, sulphur, etc. Carrageen and dillisk (dulse) are two forms of edible seaweed that have been dried and eaten for many centuries, and seaweeds are also used as a general fertilizer and for feeding to animals. Seaweed appears to confer benefits all round and, while it may at present have little to do with the iodine intake of most of us, it may well be due for fresh prominence now that plant alternatives to meat are so much in vogue. Absorption of the minerals from cereals and pulses is much improved by consumption in the same meal of fruit and vegetables. Tea and coffee hinder absorption.

Vitamins

Beefsteak is 49 per cent water, 35 per cent fat, 15.5 per cent protein and about 0.2 per cent calcium, phosphate and other minerals – a total of 99.7 per cent. The remaining fraction is comprised of vitamins. Bread, with 34 per cent water, 55 per cent carbohydrates, 8 per cent protein and 0.8 per cent fat, reaches 99.8 per cent before we can consider the mineral and vitamin content. Nevertheless, vitamins are extremely important.

Vitamins make the food we eat usable to the body for its proper functioning; they are also essential to normal metabolism; they are present in most foods; and if we lack them we suffer from deficiency diseases. They fall into two categories – fat-soluble and water-soluble. The former dissolve easily in fat, the latter in water. It is important to avoid boiling the water containing water-soluble vitamins, as this will cause the food to lose its nutritional value. Retaining the cooking-water to use in something else ensures that you do not lose the water-soluble vitamins and minerals.

Vitamin deficiency should not be found in sensible vegan, vegetarian or omnivorous diets, so their function and sources will be only briefly considered.

Vitamin A Promoting growth, skin health and contributing to the well-being of the respiratory area of the body, vitamin A comprises a group of fat-soluble compounds and is present in liver, some dairy products, vegetables and dried fruits in considerable quantities. 100 grams of raw carrots give 11,000 international units, 100 g of butter 3,300. Two ounces of fried beef liver will give you 30,280 and a cup of dried apricots 16,350, but as the day's average is 750μg retinol equivalents for a normal adult, no sleepless nights need be spent worrying about whether one is getting enough. However, as steak gives only about 15 units to 3 ounces and milk only 350 to a cup, the avid flesh-eater must be careful to eat enough of those plant foods that supply this vitamin. Equally, the health addict must be careful. In 1974 a Surrey man, reputedly a scientific adviser, ate an excessive number of vitamin A tablets and died as a result. The newspapers reported that he drank himself to death on carrot juice, but in fact the vitamin A in vegetables occurs as carotenes which the body converts into a controlled supply of the vitamin. However, excess and deficiency are both rare, though it should be remembered by flesh-eaters that there is more vitamin A in the fat of free-range animals than in many stall-fed and 'factory-farmed' beasts and birds, so milk and eggs may be a good or bad source according to the feeding methods employed.

The B vitamins Water soluble, these are very important. For proper digestion, the efficient use of fuel foods, the breaking down of proteins, for body growth and the proper maintenance of the nervous system, the B's are essential. They lose their potency through prolonged soaking or boiling, so the water used in cooking should be utilized for stock, etc., if the maximum value is to be derived. They must be taken in proportionate amounts. For example, a person who consumes a minimum amount of vitamin B_1 must have a comparable intake of B_6 in order to avoid any deficiency.

B_1 (Thiamin) The amount needed is in ratio to body-weight, physical activity and metabolic weight, but chiefly to the intake of carbohydrate. Under normal conditions 1.2 mg are enough, but, as B-group vitamins are synthesized by bowel bacteria, an antibiotic can kill the bacteria and produce a deficiency in what is apparently an adequate diet – hence the frequent prescription of vitamin B alongside a course of oral antibiotics. B_1 deficiency is also a symptom of alcoholism. Muscle tenderness, constipation, irritability and heart irregularities are among the signs of thiamin deficiency, and of course beri-beri. The best sources of thiamin are yeast, the bran and germ of cereals, pulses, beer and to a lesser extent vegetables, meat and milk. White flours often have synthetic thiamin added to compensate for the removal of the wheat germ and bran in milling. B_1 is also destroyed by sulphite food additives (E220-227.)

B_2 (Riboflavin) The energy chain processes depend upon this vitamin which, like thiamin, is derived in large quantities from yeast, but is also found in wheat germ, wholemeal flour, almonds, eggs, milk and dairy products, offal and most other foods. Cooking and heat do not harm this vitamin, and with about 1.7 mg needed daily by the adult male, there is no real excuse for being deficient in it. If one is, a dry skin and cracks in the corners of the mouth may be warning signs.

B_3 (Niacin) Niacin, nicotinic acid or nicotinamide is also necessary to produce energy. Deficiency leads to metabolic disturbances, expecially to the nervous system. Pellagra is the chief niacin-deficiency disease. Nuts, dried fruit, grain products and various other foods produce good amounts of niacin, but once again brewers' yeast and wholewheat flour are particularly good sources. 18 mg is considered adequate for an adult male and, as it is manufactured in the body from the amino acid tryptophan, a diet including adequate protein increases the total intake of niacin equivalents and makes deficiency unlikely in most Western diets.

B_6 (Pyridoxine) Apart from those dealt with above, three other vitamins of the B complex which contribute to forming the co-enzymes necessary for release of energy from fats, proteins and carbohydrates, are considered by most authorities. These are pyridoxine, pantothenic acid and biotin. Pyridoxine is widely available in vegetable foods (particularly cereals and the pulses) and animal sources. Panthothenic acid is also very plentiful. Biotin is a growth factor for many plants and animals, and is found in yeasts, liver, etc. and can be made by the bacteria in the human intestine. We need about 2,000 mg of B_6 daily and, while not everyone wants yeast every day, any more than they do liver, there is plenty in wheat germ, wholemeal bread, corn, cabbage and bananas, though very little in milk and eggs.

B_{12} (Cyanocobalamin) This vitamin is of little consequence in a lacto-vegetarian diet and today even orthodox opinion appears to be divided as to whether vegans need to worry. However, deficiency does occur, not merely in some vegans, but even more widely among flesh-eaters. No official minimum requirement appears to have been decided upon, though 3 mg daily is regarded as adequate by nutritionists. Deficiency can lead to pernicious anaemia and nervous disorders. Non-flesh sources have been listed as brewers' yeast, soya milk, wheat germ, sea kelp, yoghurt, eggs, dairy products and various prepared foods in which it is an additive. (The Vegetarian Society (UK) provides lists of supplemented foods.) The Vegan Society was for a long time very sensitive to accusations that a diet excluding all animal products might produce B_{12} deficiency symptoms and in their published literature they have considered the matter at some length (this is reviewed in Chapter 7).

Folic acid can be considered alongside B_{12} and is available in all fresh vegetables and in liver, the daily need being around 200 mg. The other members of the vitamin B complex are considered of doubtful value or rarely lacking. These are inositol, choline, para-aminobenzoic acid, citrovorum, B_{13} and B_{14}.

Vitamin C (Ascorbic acid) The best sources of this water-soluble vitamin are fruit and fresh vegetables, but it is destroyed by drying and cooking, though to a lesser extent in acid-containing foods such as tomatoes. 30 mg (NVF say 60 mg) are necessary for an adult male and this is provided by an orange or a helping of broccoli or sprouts or a few tomatoes or just any normal, sensible diet. It may help to prevent colds and is frequently deficient in elderly people who confine their diet to little but bread and tea. Vitamin C is not needed by carnivorous animals and most omni-vores and many plant-eating animals get by on a quarter or less of what our own species requires. Our need to consume the fruit and other plant life that gives us this vitamin, and to do so daily (for our bodies cannot store it), is one of the indications that man is naturally frugivorous.

Vitamin D (Cholecalciferol) Like vitamin A, this is fat-soluble and the best sources are direct sunlight, eggs, milk and butter. In its synthetic form it is widely added to such foods as margarine, but in fact most of us are independent of dietary supplies because we absorb it automatically when sunlight falls on our skins. It is the only vitamin that humans can synthesize for themselves – if they live in a good climate. Women and children of Asian descent may need supplements, as genetic differences and skin colour reduce biosynthesis and their dietary sources are poor. Large intakes can be dangerous.

Vitamin E (Tocopherol) Another fat-soluble vitamin and valuable anti-oxidant, of which we need some 20 mg daily if we are not to run the slight risk of premature birth and sterility. It is not thought that humans run much risk of deficiency and the population graph suggests that our species may be getting rather too much. It comes in such foods as egg yolk and lettuce, as well as from such sources as wheat germ, milk fat and oats. Vegetable oils provide plenty, and six tablespoons of medicinal wheat germ oil would be enough for a small army. Premature babies, missing their maternal quota, need supplements to avoid haemolytic anaemia.

Vitamin K (Menaphthone) This is a further fat-soluble vitamin needed for the clotting of blood. Most green plants and some fruits contain it and are the best sources. Lucerne (alfalfa) and spinach are particularly rich in vitamin K, though an up-to-date Popeye might equally well get his quota from the soya bean.

As the more responsible authorities make plain, only those whose diet is improperly balanced need worry about their vitamins. Babies on cow's milk may need vitamins A, C and D, however, as may some elderly people who are not looking after themselves properly. It is also acknowledged that those who subscribe to the 'whole food' philosophy have scientific fact on their side, for the sort of diet they advocate is undoubtedly richer in vitamins than are the highly processed and sophisticated mass-produced foods. Instant potato, for example, has been found to lack the vitamin C which is present in the original article. Because of the improbability of any reasonable diet providing too few vitamins, further discussion is best left to those writers whose concern is with the broader issues of nutrition.

Nevertheless, a little knowledge about nutrition – as distinct from a lot of worry, prejudice and superstition – is no bad thing, particularly for any minority subject to the baiting and half-knowledge of those for whom majority rule and conformity provide an often false sense of security. For fallacies about food are thick on the ground. As common as the erroneous belief that vegetarians don't get enough protein is the notion that butter and lard contain it or that cow's milk supplies iron or is a perfect food.[7] Most of the illusions seem to have been designed to support the habit of eating meat and animal products and it comes as a surprise to many to learn that bread and cereals supply as much protein in the average Englishman's diet as does his meat.

Another fallacy that needs to be got into perspective is that the many miserably malnourished people who are to be seen in such countries as India are evidence of the inefficacy of a vegetarian diet. The people of India – where the main dietary deficiencies are in calories, protein, calcium, iron, iodine, vitamin A and riboflavin – are largely vegetarian because they ran out of land two or three thousand years ago, for even then India was densely populated. They had no land to spare for the luxury of meat. Their religious leaders forbade animal food, with the exception of cow's milk, for this is the most economical food of animal origin, even though it needs some six to eight times more land than for bread. So the vegetarians of the East were largely compelled by economic necessity.

The superficial observer may well look at the malnourished and crippled bodies of children and adults and conclude that so pitiful a scene is evidence of the foolhardiness of cutting out animal products. There is no doubt that starving people who add some animal food to their diet, whether milk, fish or meat, are physically better off, but although a measure of animal food must of course make a poor diet more satisfactory, this is no evidence for animal food being natural to humans. Adding meat and dairy products to a poor vegetarian diet is one way of coping with the deficiency (if someone is willing to import these expensive products), but a far better way, as is now being widely realized, is to ensure instead that starving people get more of the essential proteins and vitamins from the leafy vegetables, roots, nuts and fruit to which their bodies are naturally receptive and which give the highest yields per acre of calories, protein and other nutrients and less of those starchy roots or cereals (so often refined at that) which tend to provide the bulk of the diet.

As F. A. Wilson has explained so clearly, the industrial West has not only inflicted on *itself* the refined and devitalized foods that have done so much harm. Where 'civilization' has spread, the refinery and the mill have gone too, and because the colonial people and the vast hordes of the East were already poorly fed before the white man came, his advent has meant a degree of malnutrition far worse than in the West. India, Malaya and China knew no rice mills until the Europeans came. Each Indian family had its equivalent of a pestle and mortar of wood, in which the rice was pounded and the husks broken. Then the rice was shaken in the wind on a shallow wicker trough and the husks blown away. Some of the bran also went with the wind, but enough remained to give the rice a distinctly brown colour, and much germ remained attached to the grains.

Then the rice mills and the profit-seekers came along, and rice-growing became an industry. Every bit of bran was removed and not a speck of germ remained in the starch-filled white grains. As usual, the best part went to the animals. Talc was often rubbed on to the grains to make them whiter still. As with whole and refined wheat, refined rice compares very badly with its home-pounded equivalent, known as 'paddy'. Paddy contains 13 per cent more protein and the best part of it; three times more calcium and phosphorus, twice as much iron, ninety times more vitamin A, eight times more vitamin B_1, ten times more vitamin B_2 and nearly three times more nicotinic acid. Bad as is the average European diet, the average oriental diet is far worse. On his diet of refined rice the Indian gets less than a fifth as much vitamin B_1, and less than an eighth as much vitamin A as the European. It is hardly surprising that deficiency diseases like beri-beri and blindness are so common.

It is necessary not only to show why meat and animal products are important to the human constitution, but to underline that we cannot take it for granted that our natural food is almost anything that is not derived from animals. Science and technology have helped to create such an artificial environment that even our daily bread (if that is what we should term those flabby slabs of chalk-white pap, steam-baked pre-sliced and tasteless, that many still mistake for the real thing) owes more to the chemist's laboratory than to a field of golden corn (even though the corn itself is a modern artefact of the plant-breeder). Man-cursed, the sign of bad bread was once that it had to be advertised on television. Today, many more people are eating better bread because they have accepted the virtue of a high-fibre diet.

This said, flesh-eating is the practice with which this book is concerned and, so far from it being possible to make out a sound general defence of the habit of eating pieces of animals (steak) or their surplus fluids (milk) and menstrual discharge (an egg), the dangers in so doing are probably greater than anything but a singularly unbalanced plant diet. Once we can accept this fact, and have absorbed the 'basics' of nutrition and our physiology, we should not find it difficult to settle into a dietary routine that is free of daily concern about precisely how many grams or units of this or that we are pushing down our throats. Eating and drinking can and should be a simple pleasure, given its due place and attention. Taken to excess, either in quantity or in the time we give to worrying or enthusing about it, it can lead to sickness or obsession. By all means let the whole man have whole (and humane) foods, but if he spends all his time thinking about them he may become a bore to his friends and forget about a lot of other things that are just as important and far more interesting. Balance in dealing with the subject of food is as necessary as the balance in what we actually eat.

It would not show balanced judgement, however, for the heavy meat eater to depart overnight from the eating pattern of a lifetime. If a changeover is being considered, it would be unwise to switch immediately to a diet of raw vegetables. The bugs that we carry in our intestines will not necessarily take kindly to too sudden a rejection of the meat and fish to which they have become accustomed. Their populations should be changed slowly from the putrefactive to the fermentive. Eating sour milk and plenty of fruits can help to make the transition, though merely cutting out all meat and retaining the intake of dairy products should bring nothing but benefit. Lacto-vegetarianism deprives the meat-eater of nothing his system should miss. Too sudden an alteration, however – from daily steaks to veganism, for instance – and your angry body will force your mind to cheat. Deprived too quickly of their animal products, your addicted cells will find a way of making you believe you can't do without them. Cut down on the meat and fish at once and at the same time replace them with the right non-animal foods and any craving for flesh and even dairy products will peter out.

On a more natural diet you are quite likely to lose weight if, on the old diet, you were carrying too much. This is nothing to worry about and everything to be thankful for. On a natural diet, very thin people, after losing some weight, usually begin to put it on and often find in time that they have approached a more normal weight, but it may take as much as a year or two, as weight increase is a slower business than weight reduction if excessive thinness was the result of glandular imbalance and the toxic properties of strong meats.

Children, whose lack of inclination to pounce upon the raw flesh that their mothers bring home from the shops should be evidence enough of its unsuitability, are usually more easily tempted to eat non-flesh foods than meat in any shape or form – even though family pressure has succeeded in making them accept it. The two meats to which many of us are most easily accustomed – chicken breast and bacon – are, unsurprisingly, the least representative of flesh food. The bland near-to-nothingness of the one, and the salty and more positive flavour of the other, neither of them reminding the consumer of blood and those strong juices that repel so many children – these and, one might add, the modern sausage, have more affinity with non-flesh substances such as cereal products, yeast foods and appetizers like salted peanuts than with the coarse and acquired taste of rare steak and lamb chops.

Most children will, and should, eat many vegetables raw and, although the very young often make a fuss about eating the over-cooked vegetables that appear on so many dinner plates, they do not as a rule show any resistance to eating them before they reach the cooker. Some raw vegetable foods should appear in most meals, with emphasis on salads and fruit. Raw grated vegetables and nuts can be sprinkled over cooked foods to encourage thorough chewing. There are endless variations of salads and raw vegetable dishes, and the bleak British salad of limp lettuce and an intrusion of tomato is a caricature for which no modern cook has the slightest excuse except laziness or extra-culinary overwork. Herbs, preferably fresh, can add immeasurably to the pleasure of food, though no well-run kitchen is without the biggest dried herb rack that money and space can afford. Pressure cookers and the wok are wonderful devices for cooking vegetables, ensuring a degree of nourishment and flavour never experienced by those for whom a saucepan of boiling water is the normal cooking medium for vegetables.

This is not a cookery book, but to give a broad idea of the direction menus can take the following suggestions may be helpful.

Breakfasts are best based on fruits and that combination of cereals, nuts, dried fruit, etc., that is known on the continent as muesli and has become much more popular of late in prepared, packeted form, available under various brand names in virtually every grocers and supermarket. Wholemeal bread with the various nut butters, margarines and one or other of the now widely available 'spreads' are extremely sustaining and very palatable.

After an adequate breakfast on such lines (and if you think cornflakes and bacon are more sustaining, you are the victim more of belief than of experience!), a light lunch – if you have your main meal in the evening – in which salads and fruit predominate will keep both mind and body far more alert than those high-protein and stodgy meals with which too many of us end our useful work period before the day has got properly into its stride.

The main meal of the day should provide the bulk of the needed protein, and whether this is to be strictly vegetarian (in which case nuts, most legumes and grain foods provide what is needed) or lacto-vegetarian (the high protein content of most hard cheeses beats meat any time), the variety that may be introduced into such a diet usually astonishes those who previously believed that a meat-based diet gave greater choice. The opposite is the case, as any good vegetarian cookery book makes clear. In point of fact, many omnivorous diets are boring and monotonous in the extreme, and the unadventurous, 'typically English' meat-and-two-veg notion of culinary craftsmanship is surely the all-time nutritional low. There is something slightly pathetic about the ease with which many of us are conned by habit and the advertisers into believing that a portion of blanket-like factory-farmed chicken set off against a small pile of frozen peas and some over-boiled peeled potatoes, is hitting the double-top of *haute cuisine*.

Finally, and with no apology, I repeat that a balanced attitude to nutrition is what is needed, but do not be deluded by the sophistry of those who twist this to support the spurious nonsense of 'a little of what you fancy does you good'. A little of what we fancy may not do us so much harm that it should be avoided at all costs, but the fact remains that if what we are putting into our bodies is foreign to their chemistry, we are to that extent poisoning ourselves, whether what we fancy is the smoke of a single cigarette, a grain of arsenic or a lump of decomposing flesh. Balance in nutrition should be as between good and good, not good and bad. Balance for the human species is not eating flesh *and* plant life, but combining the various forms of the latter to create a balanced diet. Despite the many artifices, equivocations, back-pedallings and wishful thoughts with which most of us resist any pressure to do the thing that should come naturally and with the maximum benefit to ourselves as well as to the animals we exploit, it really is as easy as that. The proof, however, can only be in the eating.

Notes

1. Wide variations are available. Powdered soya milk contains approximately 22.5 per cent protein (2.8 per cent for 1 to 7 dilution), 46.8 per cent carbohydrate (5.9 per cent), 22.6 per cent fat (2.8 per cent), 4.2 per cent ash (0.5 per cent), 3.9 per cent moisture (88.0 per cent), an ounce of the powder providing 136 calories and 100 i.u. of vitamin D. Whole dried cow's milk in the (MN) tables supplies 26.6 per cent protein, 37.6 per cent carbohydrate, 27.7 per cent fat, and approximately the same number of calories.

2. The idea that 'first class' protein was found only in meat was knocked on the head as long ago as 1955 when *The Extra Pharmacopoeia* announced: 'The terms first and second class protein came into being in the first World War and were based on incomplete analyses of pure protein and on inadequate experiments on rats ... the terms have now become meaningless and should be discarded.' Many other authorities have made similar statements (e.g., *Mind and Body*, vol. 6, page 2277, Orbis, 1973; Davidson, *The Principles and Practice of Medicine*, page 413, sixth edition, E. & S. Livingstone, 1963). Tofu, tempeh, etc., are now readily available forms of high protein, and mycoprotein savoury pies, though not wholly vegetarian, are superceding products using TVP as an ingredient.

    The capacity of proteins of different origin to make good one another's deficiencies when they are consumed together is known as their *supplementary value*.

3. Kitchen garden enthusiasts can now grow soya beans successfully in Great Britain. Some varieties raised in the south and south-east of Sweden can be satisfactorily grown in northern Europe. North America, producing over three-quarters of the world's supply grown for animal feeds, has no problem – the Middle West is on the same latitude as Manchuria, the birthplace of the soya bean. Sown in mid-May in Britain it can be cropped green (to be eaten like runner beans) during August, or shelled for dried beans by the end of

September. For those who wish to get the flavour and texture of meat without condoning the cruelty and health hazards that go with it, meat analogues derived from soya or broad beans with added vegetable (typically palm) oil, containing a negligible amount of cholesterol, can fool the most dyed-in-the-wool flesh-addict. In pet foods, of course, TVPs have already gained a firm foothold and can replace real meat for dogs and to some extent, cats – at a consequent cost saving. The soya bean should not be confused with the field bean(*Vicia faba*), which is still primarily an animal feed. Low in carbohydrate, yet high in calories, the 'acclimatized' soya bean is approximately 40 per cent protein and an excellent source of vitamins A, B_1, C and G; also of calcium, iron and phosphorous. Its small starch content has commended it to diabetics. It is interesting to compare the green bean with its 'textured' relative. 'Protoveg', for instance, provides between 19 and 23 calories per ounce hydrated against 65 calories per ounce in minced beef. Protein is 15.7 per cent, fat 0.6 per cent, crude fibre 3 per cent, minerals 6.3 per cent. Although the 'Protoveg' analysis shows 31.5 per cent carbohydrates, the greater proportion is non-metabolizable, i.e., dietary fibre.

4. 'Gelatine and certain vegetable proteins are deficient in some of the essential amino acids, but a mixed vegetable diet, including pulses, can supply enough of all.' Davidson, *The Principles and Practice of Medicine*, page 413, sixth edition, E. & S. Livingstone.

5. If silviculture becomes part of the diversification brought about by EEC surpluses, nut-bearing trees may yet play their part in a more sane agriculture.

6. After stating that a 70 kg man can maintain nitrogen equilibrium on 32 g protein per day, D. S. Miller has said: · . . the vulnerable groups in society are the toddlers and the lactating mother. Adult man can indeed live on bread alone and protein-rich foods should be directed towards his wife and children.' *Proceedings of the Royal Society of Medicine*, vol. 60, November, 1967.

Although the outcome of the United Nations World Food Conference in 1974 left much to be desired, its debate on the international food crisis prompted renewed attention from many quarters, ranging from such admissions from nutritionists that even 2,800 calories and 65 g of protein may be far more than most of us need, to forthright statements from economists on the sheer wastefulness of rearing animals for human food.

Experiments on university athletes and men in the United States Army have shown that an actual reduction in protein intake results in a marked improvement of physical performance. This contrasts sharply with the long-held idea that athletes need vast quantities of meat. Many athletic records have been held by vegetarians, including Olympic medals being won for running, swimming, etc. See Rudd: *Why Kill for Food?* et al.

7. Cow's milk contains almost no iron and would cause anaemia as a sole diet. It is almost completely lacking in vitamin C. It has value for infants and children lacking anything better, but adults can obtain too much of the wrong kind of fat from it.

CHAPTER 7

The further step

A vegetarian diet is the acid test of humanitarianism.
Leo Tolstoy

The unlimited capacity of the plant world to sustain man at his highest is a region yet unexplored by modern science . . . I submit that scientists have not yet explored the hidden possibilities of the innumerable seeds, leaves and fruits for giving the fullest possible nutrition to mankind.
Mahatma Gandhi, quoted by Tendulkar, 1944

The role of plant foods relative to that of animal foods in human nutrition is one of the most crucial questions . . . plants have constituted and will constitute the major part of the daily food of the developing countries, contributing as they do nine tenths of their calorie and protein supply.
Dr Boerma, Director General
Food and Agriculture Organization of the United Nations,
Plant Foods for Human Nutrition, 1968

Flesh-eating is not necessary to health.
Encyclopaedia Britannica, 1973

You have just dined, and however scrupulously the slaughter-house is concealed in the graceful distance of miles, there is complicity.
Ralph Waldo Emerson, *Fate*

I am in favour of animal rights as well as human rights. That is the way of a whole human being.
Abraham Lincoln, *Complete Works*

Throughout the history of mankind, or at least since the agricultural revolution, the vast majority of our species has lived on little but grain. It seems absurd, therefore, that so many of us should regard veganism – with the excellent variety of foods it can offer – as a daring departure from the norm. With domestic animals eating up to ten times as much of the Earth's primary plant food as humans, and the problems of mal-nourishment and actual starvation greater than ever before, a serious world-wide study of the principles and practicability of vegan nutrition would be a responsible and reasonable measure wholly in line with current awareness of mankind's predicament.

Nonetheless, for the majority of omnivorous Westerners it is enough to make the first move the adoption of a lacto-vegetarian diet, though we cannot forever shut our eyes to the fact that the further step of veganism may well come from necessity if not from choice, for the simple reason that the meat and dairy industries are inseparably linked luxuries it is becoming increasingly difficult to afford.

The logic of the vegan case is absolute. No one – whether nutritionist, physician, sociologist or layman – can rebut the veganic argument in any important respect. Veganism is part of the most truly civilized concept of life of which the human mind has been capable. More than ordinary lacto-vegetarianism, veganism 'speaks to the condition' of our modern world. That only a minute number of Western people puts its principles into practice is evidence of nothing but our reluctance to break with habit and to put conscience before the social inconveniences of a pattern of life that is foreign to the bulk of the society in which we live, yet it is inseparable from that holistic vision that is at last beginning to take hold.

The objections to veganism, then, are selfish rather than rational. It is only fair to a courageous minority to make this quite clear and I can say this because I am myself one of the many who *know* better than they *do*. I am not yet the fully consistent vegan I would like to be, and let it be remembered that total consistency is impossible. The pressures on most of us not to go the whole way are tremendous and, in many a family, sadly divisive. There must be numerous vegetarians who, in doubt and with despondency, have compromised their principles for the sake of a quieter or more workable life, perhaps putting an outwardly more harmonious background for the children or their work before the obligation they feel in their hearts they owe to the world outside the closed circle of family. Whether the tension that can result is any easier to cope with than the social sacrifices demanded by greater consistency is something that can only be answered individually.

At first sight there is little in the veganic argument that is different from that of the lacto-vegetarian's. Reverence for life, environmental responsibility, man's physical and spiritual development – vegans and vegetarians share these concerns with equal conviction, but it has to be said that vegans show a more logical and consistent approach because of their practical acceptance of the fact that we cannot consume eggs and dairy products without tacitly supporting the ceaseless cruelty that is as related to the production of milk, butter, cheese, eggs and the many foods in which they are used as to the actual pieces of flesh which are where the lacto-vegetarian draws his line.[1]

It is not possible, or at least not practicable, to produce milk and milk products without subjecting both cow and calf to the full range of procedures, culminating in slaughter, that govern the life of domesticated cattle. Cows have to be subjected to yearly pregnancies so that the milk, cheese and cream that form a substantial part of the diet of both lacto-vegetarians and meat-eaters may be produced. Many imagine that the cow is only relieved of her surplus milk after her calf has been satisfied, but hardly any cows in dairy herds are allowed to suckle their calves for more than three days if at all. Dairy calves are now nearly always reared by hand so that the milk which the cow provides can be sold. 'Separating the calf from the mother shortly after birth undoubtedly inflicts anguish on both. Cattle are highly intelligent, and attachment between the calf and the mother is particularly strong.' (*Report of the Brambell Committee*, HMSO, 1965.)

The calves, the inevitable by-product of the continual pregnancies that are necessary to keep a cow producing milk, have several possible fates. They may go to slaughter almost immediately, their few brief hours of life involving separation from their mother, transport in trucks to market and further handling and movement before their butchers turn them into veal and ham pies and drain their stomachs of the rennet that is used to make most commercial cheeses.

If they go to a white veal unit they will spend the rest of their lives tethered in narrow crates, deprived of water except in the specially designed slop with which they are fed, kept short of iron (to produce the white meat that is the sign of anaemia demanded by the public for this vilely procured product) and given little if any of the roughage that their special digestive systems as ruminants require. Often reduced to eating their own hair and nibbling their crates, they are denied even the comfort of bedding because their craving for solid food would tempt them to eat it. Many emerge from their crates at the end of their fourteen weeks of existence suffering from stomach ulcers and abscesses and too weak to stand in the slaughter-house lorries. 'Calves at large', said the Brambell Report, 'are normally active and playful animals.' So are human children, given the chance. When we are as concerned for the 'battered babies' of other species as we are for our own, we shall have learned to substitute the logic of civilized mankind for the insensitivity of savages. Thankfully, in Britain, crate-rearing of veal calves is giving way to new systems that should alleviate some of the abuses.

Some 70 per cent of the beef produced is a by-product of the dairy industry, and calves from beef herds often have a comparatively tolerable fate, being allowed to suck, to run with their dams and to graze in the fields until the time comes for the fattening pens and the slaughter-house, but the surplus calves from the dairy herds are frequently sent to market when a week old (or less) and bought for rearing in intensive beef units if not immediately slaughtered.

In these days of artificial insemination, few 'bobby' calves are reared as bulls and for the exceptions life will be largely one of solitary confinement with interludes serving real or artificial cows and rubber tubes. Owing to the trend for dual-purpose breeding, fewer bobbies are being slaughtered than before, but their continued marketing has brought much criticism from the Farm Animal Welfare Council. If female, the calves may be thought suitable to rear as dairy cows, in which case they are removed as soon after birth as possible so that the cow 'may settle down again in the herd'. That is, she is granted the minimum time to get over the strain of her frustrated pregnancies so that her milk can as soon as possible go to produce the all-important profits. Fed on milk substitutes, the calves' development is encouraged so that at 18-24 months they too can begin the cycle of continuous pregnancies.

As *The New Scientist* (13 January, 1972) admits, 'The modern dairy cow leads a hell of a life. Each year she hopefully produces a calf which means that for nine months of the year she is pregnant. And for nine months of each year she is milked twice a day. For six months she is both pregnant and lactating.' Fifteen years on, with such techniques as multiple ovulation, embryo transfer, routine Caesarians, and slaughter during pregnancy, her sufferings are anything but diminished. Details of the ailments she can succumb to while meeting these demands make disquieting reading, as do the remedies employed. Giving birth is often a prolonged and painful business for the cow, to be rewarded only by separation from her baby. A cow often cries out and searches for her calf for days after it is taken away. When after years of exploitation her milk yield drops, she is sent to the slaughter-house before profit turns into loss. As worn-out cow's meat is not popular in Britain, countless thousands of animals have been sent abroad for slaughter. The hideous cruelty found in continental abattoirs is too well-known to need repeating here and has for some time been a target for those who don't wish to give up eating meat, but, conscience partly awakened, are able to deceive themselves and others that if only our animals don't get their throats cut by foreigners, everything will be seen to be for the best in the best of all possible worlds.

For some animals in some parts of the world the so-called 'humane' killer is employed, but that is the most one can say. For countless millions of creatures every single day brings a brutal and painful death unrelieved by even token attempts to lessen their sufferings. Even where the humane killer is used, the attendant circumstances of often long-distance transport, rough handling, food withheld before slaughter, the terror of the waiting within the smell of blood suffered by many creatures and the violence in their handling at the hands of men whose concern for the feelings of the overfamiliar objects of their livelihoods has inevitably been eradicated – these are all factors inseparable from the whole brutal and squalid business. The FAWC reports on slaughtering and ritual methods leave no doubt about the obscenities we are prepared to inflict under the banner of 'science' and 'progress'.

As K. Jannaway has written (*What Happens to the Cow and Her Calf?*, Movement for Compassionate Living – the Vegan Way, 1985): 'All this to produce food for humans that is not necessary! Human babies should have their mother's milk, and children and adults the solid food appropriate to their dentition and digestive systems. These can easily be selected from richly varied plant sources. For babies and children where necessary or desired, and for invalids or those who still like to take milk ... nutritious plant milks are available ... The dairy industry is inseparable from the cruel exploitation and degradation of helpless, highly intelligent animals.'

Egg production is also unacceptable to vegans because it involves the virtually unavoidable necessity to slaughter the male birds and insufficiently productive hens. Modern techniques with their battery and broiler systems, unnatural feeding, selective breeding and perverse methods of laying stimulation constitute continual ruthless exploitation. The cruelty and carelessness in the slaughter of chickens whether at the hands of the back-yard neck-wringer or on the conveyor belts of slaughtering plants, is as well-known and as obvious as the absence of public concern. The majority of us are successful in forgetting or ignoring even the furthest extremes of brutality if the alternative is to give up the sacrosanct slices and by-products of animals that we insist upon consuming, and it is useless to salve one's conscience with the notion that the physical and psychological torments of animals can be remedied by adjustments and modifications. As Kath Clements reminds us in *Why Vegan?*, through exposure, starvation, drug side-effects, bad husbandry and sheer neglect, some 16,000 large animals die 'unnecessarily' every day on British farms (*The Veterinary Record*, vol. III, no. 2, 1982):

> Farming methods account for many more animals' deaths by accident than vivisection does by design. Veterinary supervision is not required by law in treatment of farm animals despite the massive reliance by farmers on medication, so that most vets these days make their livings from the more profitable household pets industry. A farm is the last place on Earth where a true animal-lover would feel at home.

Nor should the magic words 'free range' calm our unease. Vegetarian egg-eaters tend to forget that hens, like cows, produce male offspring in equal numbers to the females. For nearly every laying hen, a male chick has had to be slaughtered.

> The details of this, in modern hatcheries, are not very pleasant. No rules govern their slaughter, since they are not destined for human consumption. After sexing, the unlucky males are sometimes thrown live into a mincer, to convert them into feedstuff, sometimes simply thrown into polythene bags to suffocate *en masse*. The chicks destined for the broilerhouse are hardly less fortunate. People who salve their conscience by eating only free-range eggs forget that this side of the business is an integral part of egg production. (Kath Clements, *Why Vegan?*)

There is no remedy for animal suffering except to stop breeding and eating other forms of sentient life. All half-measures are mere self-deception, as is the notion that we can keep omnivorous 'pets' and still be 'animal lovers'. To feed one animal on the dead flesh of other equally intelligent and sensitive creatures, is to be as much part and parcel of the 'system' as to serve behind a butcher's counter. We must learn to accept that other creatures' lives and liberty are not for our convenience and pleasure. A hard lesson for many, admittedly, but one we cannot afford to shirk.

Though we may be far from seeing such a vision realized, it cannot be denied that the adoption of a vegan diet throughout the world would not only release the huge areas of land now being used for animal exploitation, but would involve the right care of the land and its best use to satisfy the real needs of man and other forms of life. However, this argument has already been explored and, while it is tempting to discuss other aspects of the vegan régime (which embraces clothing, cosmetics, sport and those other spheres of daily life that involve the misuse of animals), such investigations must be left to those who wish to take the matter further. Those who do will discover that a consistent lifestyle is by no means easily achieved. As Nigel Dudley, author of *This Poisoned Earth*, pointed out in his 1987 Frey Ellis Memorial Lecture, 'the lives saved by adopting a vegan diet are no more than a tiny fraction of the animals killed to provide vegetable food by conventional farming methods. A vegan diet which is not also an organic diet is totally illogical and a requirement to eat organic food should be adopted as a central part of a vegan philosophy.'

Vitamin B_{12} The only serious criticism that has been made of veganism relates to possible deficiency in vitamin B_{12}. In the present state of knowledge it is a little difficult to know just how much of the problem – if problem there be – to present in this context. Medical and nutritionists' opinions are far from unanimous and there are some puzzling contradictions. The matter has not been simplified by the realization that B_{12} deficiency is even more prevalent among meat-eaters than among vegans. Some recent research, indeed, has prompted the suggestion that its rare incidence among vegans – as being *due* to their veganism – is in doubt. The medical dictionary *Mind and Body* (Orbis, 1973) has already been quoted on this point (see page 82) and study of the medical journals provides ample evidence of deficiency among those whose nutritional standards would seem to be adequate. 'Vitamin B_{12} deficiency is a commoner cause of mental illness among omnivores than is generally believed', it was stated in a leading article in *The Lancet* (ii, 309, 1969), 'and screening of all psychiatric patients for pernicious anaemia associated with such deficiency has been advocated.'

Lack of vitamin B_{12}, then, can cause illness and in rare cases even death. It should be understood, however, that the same can be said of other nutritional scarcities (and excesses) and that B_{12} deficiency does not necessarily indicate that the patient has failed to consume the quantity considered to be adequate. He can eat the vitamin without his body being able to utilize it. What causes this intestinal ineptitude is as much in doubt as are such basic data as the minimal daily amount of B_{12} required by the human body. In fairness to nutritional experts, however, B_{12} was isolated only as recently as 1948, which in biochemical terms is no great while ago.

It is interesting and possibly very relevant that lifelong vegans seldom suffer from B_{12} deficiency. Where deficiency in vegans has been established, it has been mostly in people who have switched, perhaps too abruptly, from a diet based on animal products. This has helped to prompt the suspicion that as children brought up from birth on a vegan diet are able to absorb the B_{12} made by the bacteria in their colons, it may be that the perversion of the body's chemistry through meat-eating has made it impossible for a small number of people to switch to the more natural vegan diet later in life without showing signs of B_{12} deficiency.[2]

This is not to say, of course, that symptoms due to inadequate *intake* of B_{12} are not to be found in malnourished people the world over, whether they are omnivorous or more selective in their eating habits. An inadequate diet will be deficient in a great many elements, whether or not meat is included. Although volumes have been written about B_{12}, it is in our knowledge of man's adaptational abilities that we have far to go; the uncertainties surrounding a clearly inadequate intake (irrespective of absorptional capacity) are less in dispute.

It is known that the bacteria in the human colon synthesize B_{12}, but that in most cases this is not available for absorption by the large intestine because the absorption takes place in the lower end of the ileum (or small intestine). This absorption depends, in part, upon the presence of the 'intrinsic factor', a protein-like substance produced in the stomach. In the case of pernicious anaemia, for instance, this intrinsic factor is absent. There is some evidence that the large intestine of vegans can absorb B_{12} (Ellis, F. R.; Wokes, F., 'Vitamin B_{12}', *The Vegan*, Winter, 1966/67) – a point that may well be given more prominence as research continues.

Another point that has received some attention and has tended to confuse the issue, at least for the layman, is that vegans are prone to 'abnormal' electroencephalograms. The reason for this is in doubt, but 'is almost certainly not related to vitamin B_{12} deficiency' (Ellis, F. R.; Montegriffo, V. M .E., 'The Health of Vegans', *Plant Foods for Human Nutrition*, vol. 2, no. 2, January, 1971). However, disagreement and partial knowledge surround this finding and in view of the link that some have suggested it might be reasonable for the intrepid layman to question the basic assumption of abnormality. For if that 'abnormality' is being judged by chemical differences from those who eat animal products, it seems logical to suppose that healthy (and so presumably fully adjusted) vegans' (and other higher primates'?) EEGs are normal, but that meat-eaters' are not. What is normality? A blood chemistry that is the result of centuries of persistent wrong feeding and unnatural living conditions, or the state of equilibrium for which our species was designed? The answer seems obvious, the question almost absurd, yet allopathic medicine itself is based on the appallingly unscientific absurdity of dosing the symptoms of our unnatural habits with poisons instead of promulgating the fundamental need to obey those rules that are the only guarantee of good, or at least improved, health.

It may be asked whether gorillas and other primates living in natural surroundings and eating what they instinctively choose have 'EEG abnormality'. There certainly seems to be no reason to suppose that any of them suffer from B_{12} deficiency. Dr E. Lester Smith and others have suggested that apes in the wild get their fair share simply because they pick it up from excreta and other such bonuses about which they are not overfastidious. I am not qualified to argue in scientific terms with such distinguished authorities, but it is difficult to suppress the feeling that nature must have found a less haphazard way of ensuring that the apes get what they need. Primitive man, it follows, did not suffer from any undue obsession with hygiene and therefore got along all right, but plenty of modern men are also none too fussy and it does not seem to have been established that B_{12} deficiency is confined to the nanny-trained and clinically pernickety members of the human community.

It is not a problem that can be solved by studying the EEG's and B_{12} levels in apes, because although it is known that some species of monkeys kept in captivity on a clean vegan diet can suffer from B_{12} deficiency, it is also known that it is not possible to draw accurate and relevant conclusions from the study of organisms removed from their natural habitat – a fact that forms one of the biggest scientific arguments against animal experiments. B_{12} deficiency in a captive monkey living on sterilized nuts is not proof that cleanliness has caused the deficiency. Not, that is, cleanliness *per se*. Stress – whether from wrong feeding, noise, fear, imprisonment, boredom or any other result of upsetting an organism's normal pattern and rhythm of life – invalidates almost every conclusion drawn from study of creatures in captive and unnatural conditions.

Looking at the B_{12} question objectively and in the light of what little is really known rather than conjectured, it does seem improbable in view of man's chemical and physiological similarity to the higher primates that vegans should fail to get enough B_{12} in a diet that befits their nearest known relatives; it seems more likely that if the puzzle has a chemical answer, it may be the freshness and instinctive choice of an ape's food that gives him what some vegans and omnivores lack. The fact that meat-eaters can also suffer from B_{12} deficiency makes it impossible to assert that actual lack of intake of B_{12} in human food is necessarily responsible, and I believe it is therefore more reasonable to give less attention to dietetic shortage of B_{12} than to the fundamental reasons for individual inability to benefit from the probably very small amount man needs for his proper functioning.

It seems, indeed, reasonable to pursue the possibility that the physical and nervous complications attributed to B_{12} deficiency have much more to do with the nature of our civilized lives than with the need for a vitamin in amounts in excess of what is sufficient for the other primates. This must, as implied, leave open-ended the question of whether the freshness and choice factors are crucial, but pending any more conclusive findings in this field we might do better to seek to understand B_{12} deficiency and many other ills in the light of, and in proportion to, our general departure from an environment and way of life that would be consistent with our physical structure.

If a diet free of all animal products is for most vegans perfectly adequate, then for such people it can presumably be rightly termed 'natural'. Possibly they have simply not been thrown into so unnatural a balance as have meat-eaters and those vegans who depend upon excessive(?) quantities of B_{12}. It may be found that we should be working on the assumption not that we need so much B_{12}, but that we *don't* need something else: as suggested, civilization or some nutrient or combination of modern refined foods that is acting against either the natural synthesizing of B_{12} in the human body or the truly healthy and uncontaminated organism's ability to function without B_{12}. Dr Lester Smith's observation that although controversy persists as to the occurrence of B_{12} in higher plants, there is enough to be nutritionally significant in foodstuffs consumed in large quantities (Smith, E. Lester, *Vitamin B_{12}*, Methuen, 1965), suggests that herbivorous and frugivorous species should not need a higher intake of the vitamin than they will absorb from their normal diet.

In general, it should be noted, the health of vegans is good (Ellis F. R.; Montegriffo, V. M. E., op. cit.), as might be expected among people whose body-weight is lighter than average, whose cholesterol and blood urea levels are lower, and whose consumption of more fibrous food than is usual among flesh-eaters almost certainly diminishes the likelihood of developing those various and often serious diseases to which the overloaded and frequently costive systems of many meat-eaters are prone. But absorption problems are complicated and cannot properly be dealt with here, so I am not attempting to argue against those scientists whose knowledge in this field is far greater than my own, but rather – accepting that scientists themselves are still far from agreement – to review some of the salient points and suggest a change of emphasis. None of the great men of science would deny that specialists often work from incorrect or insufficiently broad assumptions. In this instance, perhaps the questionable assumption concerns what may be fairly regarded as the norm. As the incidence of B_{12} deficiency symptoms in vegans is very small, and is also found in omnivores with seemingly adequate B_{12} intake, it is perhaps time that research into the problem became far more fundamental. I believe the answers may be found when there is a greater balance, a more profound recognition of those laws by which this planet's total ecology is governed and to which mankind is no exception. Although it might well be wise for people who are changing from a meat-based diet to a vegan diet to take B_{12} supplements, as a way of reducing the possible shock to the system, this is not an admission or evidence that our species inherently needs to add to the B_{12} found naturally in plant life; rather, it suggests that having thrown our chemistry 'out of gear' we should be cautious in moving towards a more natural and sane way of life (imprisoned men have resisted their first taste of freedom and sunlight). That sanity, I am quite convinced, cannot be established while we maintain an exploitative, unscientific and profoundly selfish attitude to our total environment.

Notes

1. Half measures always produce problems of where to draw the line. The lacto-vegetarian whose concern is primarily with the cruelty aspect is in a particularly difficult position. Although the definition of a vegetarian that is accepted by the British and most other vegetarian societies is one who abstains from the use of flesh, fish and fowl, with or without the addition of eggs and dairy produce', the problem remains, for those who wish to face it, of deciding whether the greater cruelty lies in the eating of eggs and dairy products, or fish. Neither an egg nor a piece of cheese is in itself so obviously

related to a sentient victim as is a dead herring, complete from head to tail. A wild pigeon who leaves an egg on my cabbage patch will not find me spurning her offering on the grounds of conscience, though I'd prefer the cabbage. Is there most suffering involved in eating a kipper, an omelette or a fondu? How do we assess the element of suffering? Is the coldness of a fish's blood a clue to the degree of suffering involved in its death? On the other hand, what is it like to 'drown' in the air and how many fish are gutted while still alive on board the factory ships? When one considers that a single hen will produce some hundreds of eggs in her lifetime, should one 'divide' the suffering in her life and death by the number of eggs she has produced in order to arrive at the pain-content of a single egg? Equally, should one 'divide' the suffering of a cow and her calves by the pounds and gallons of butter, cheese and milk that the cow's life-span has produced? I know this begins to sound ridiculous to many people, but the lacto-vegetarian is not on firm ground in stopping short of veganism and he could achieve greater consistency by examining and deciding upon such considerations individually. Some may calculate that, despite the definition of vegetarianism that has been quoted, it may be the lesser of two evils to eat fish (or perhaps just some fish) than eggs or dairy produce. Only the vegan can afford to ignore the question.

2. To put the horse more squarely before the cart, there is a good deal of support for the theory that man lost his ability to manage with dietary B_{12} when he took to meat-eating, which caused the bacterium *Escherichia coli* to move further down his intestinal tract to beyond the point at which the B_{12} could be absorbed (see A. G. Long and F. Wokes, 'Vitamins and Minerals in Plants', *Plant Foods for Human Nutrition*, Vol. 1, No. 1, May, 1968). The upward movement of the *Escherichia*, it may be, is encouraged by a return to that vegan pattern we abandoned. However, the inner reaches of our intestines are not of universal fascination and most of us prefer to leave the problems of bacterial balance to the scientists. I must leave it to the really keen reader to explore this for himself in greater depth.

3. Space does not allow for a full examination of the many forms of suffering caused to birds and animals by our insistence on eating their bodies. Compassion in World Farming (20 Lavant Street, Petersfield, Hampshire GU32 3EW) cover every aspect of farming and slaughtering methods in their excellent journal *Agscene*.

CHAPTER 8

Human or humane?

The extraordinary thing about the modern 'life sciences' is that they hardly ever deal with life as such, *the factor x, but devote infinite attention to the study and analysis of the physico-chemical body that is life's carrier . . . there is no excuse for the pretence that life is nothing but physics and chemistry.*

Nor is there any excuse for the pretence that consciousness is nothing but a property of life. To describe an animal as a physico-chemical system of extreme complexity is no doubt perfectly correct, except that it misses out on the 'animalness' of the animal. Some zoologists, at least, have advanced beyond this level of erudite absurdity and have developed an ability to see animals as more than complex machines. Their influence, however, is as yet deplorably small, and with the increasing 'rationalization' of the modern lifestyle, more and more animals are being treated as if they really were nothing but 'animal machines'.

E. F. Schumacher, *A Guide for the Perplexed*

That the predatory way of life is still observed by newer forms of life is in its measure an indictment against them. It is in principle a status quo persisted in after becoming due to disappear. 'Might is right' as a principle in the newest phase of life would seem doomed because it exemplifies in principle a status quo. Therefore, that predaceous man has an immensely long tradition behind him is no sanction for him; it may be an excuse, but it is no authorization; it would authorize anachronism. It would seem that homo praedatorious *is in a backwater unreached by the tide which set in some millennia since.*

What is it then that poisons Nature? The cruelty of life . . . In (man) evolving mind has got so far as to become critical of life. He feels the curse as well as the blessing attached to 'zest-to-live'. He is impressed by a cruelty inherent in the economy of life. He is disillusioned the more to find he is a part of that same dispensation. The regime is, if he asks his 'heart', one for which he cannot seek his heart's approval.

Sir Charles Sherrington, *Man on his Nature*

. . . the cruelty that goes on under the barbarous régime we call civilization.

Thomas Hardy in a letter to Florence Henneker
on man's treatment of animals

The great discovery of the nineteenth century, that we are of one blood with the lower animals, has created new ethical obligations which have not yet penetrated the public conscience. The clerical profession has been lamentably remiss in preaching this obvious duty.

Dean Inge

They sniffed, poor things, for their green fields,
They cried so loud I could not sleep;
For fifty thousand shillings down
I would not sail again with sheep.

W. H. Davies

The unpardonable forgetfulness in which the lower animals have hitherto been left by the moralists of Europe is well known. It is pretended that the beasts have no rights. They persuade themselves that our conduct in regard to them has nothing to do with morals or (to speak the language of their morality) that we have no duties towards animals; a doctrine revolting, gross and barbarous . . .

Arthur Schopenhauer

Before the first word of this book was written, a final chapter was planned to consist of precise details of some of the many cruelties our species inflicts on those edible creatures we sacrifice daily and in vast numbers to our uncaring greed and cowardice. Volumes could be produced to support the moral, compassionate and aesthetic reasons for moving from an animal economy to one based on plant life. Endless stomach-turning, mind-sickening, even heart-touching examples could be quoted of the torments that are inflicted upon fear-knowing, pain-feeling living beings – torments that we know only too well go on, but of which we do not wish to receive uncomfortable reminders. Yet it would not be an original exercise to list mankind's brutalities. Many have done so and their works for the most part have been respectfully received or silently ignored and then forgotten. To quote cruelty as a basis for reform may be pardonable but it seldom gets attention.

It is more realistic, perhaps, *not* to concentrate for too long on the barbarities that anyone who thinks knows perfectly well are going on incessantly. It would be easy enough to paint in all too accurately strong colours a picture of, for instance, calves born without the will to live or even to suck ('liveability' is an example of farming newspeak) – many of them lucky (if that is the word) if they are allowed more than two or three days to live at all; to convey some measure of the physical agony experienced by the two million whales, dolphins and porpoises slaughtered in the past fifty years with such brutality, for products obtainable from plant and mineral sources; to invite pity for the prolapsed hen dragging her guts around (if permitted the freedom to walk) until she dies of weakness or cannibalism; to stress that (to take only a single statistic) 450 million poultry are slaughtered every year in Great Britain alone; to point to the fact that pigs can literally die of fright prior to slaughter – a danger so well known to farmers that they will feed them linseed meal or vitamin E medicines, lack of vitamin E being associated with myocardial infarction (heart attack); to add that thousands of millions of this, that or the other specially bred animal or bird are slaughtered yearly so that a proportion of the human species can continue to eat what it wants but does not need; to condemn the vested interests that have latched on to the farmers' rapacity, offering a range of powerful drugs not under the supervision of a vet or a doctor and marketed solely by the persuasion of merchants, regardless of their suitability and side-effects; to suggest that we hide our slaughter-houses and other centres of animal suffering behind high walls and in out-of-the-way places precisely because we know only too well what is necessary if we are to indulge our greed; to emphasize that in pressing for the abolition or moderation of 'factory-farming methods' – as do organizations that have done such sincerely motivated good work as Compassion in World Farming – we are in danger of deceiving ourselves that controlled, reduced or alternative cruelty is adequate concession to humane conscience; to argue at length that not only have other creatures a right to live but (and more to the point within a system that breeds domesticated species solely for consumption of their flesh and by-products) they have the even more critical right not to be born at all at the whim of man; to prove, in short, that in our half-baked thinking and incessant ferocity towards the countless sentient creatures whom, alive, we imprison, mutilate, maim, trap, strangle, shoot, hook, chase, snare, de-limb, behead, suffocate, flay, disembowel, stab, crush, force-feed, burn, drown, boil, freeze, cut up, make sick, terrorize and by numerous other means mercilessly exploit day in and day out for no better reason than that we wish to devour them, we are shamefully forsaking that one obligation which, above all others, we should recognize – to put our unique knowledge of the difference between good and evil, between mercy and cruelty, before our heart-hardening greed.[1]

It is relevant and interesting to compare the articles on slaughtering that have appeared in the *Encyclopaedia Britannica* over the past 100 years. In the 9th edition (1875), under 'Abattoir', can be found two pages of explicit description, showing a taking-it-for-granted insensitivity towards the least savoury of trades. In each edition since, the matter is given less prominence, both in graphic detail and in length. The most recent edition has almost phased out the subject altogether, relegating it to a sub-heading under 'meat and meat-packing'. It is significant, perhaps, that so prominent a growth industry should receive such declining attention. Is it more realistic to attribute this to a growing sense of shame than to an increase in callous indifference? The question must be left open.

It would seem as pointless to go into greater details of our abominable behaviour towards the other creatures with whom we share this planet as it would be to elaborate on the statistics of *human* suffering and misery – with the figures for cruelty to children, for instance, which are of no less concern to those who have faced up to the totality of men's savagery. For it is not just the known numbers of babies and young boys and girls who are physically and visibly assaulted by brutalized adults that are so appalling, but also the incalculable number of cases where all that greed and selfishness is directed in innumerable less overt ways against young creatures towards whom we should be most expected to direct our love and concern.

Easy as it would be to draw the parallel at considerable length, what good would be done? Those who already know what we do, either care or don't care. No amount of proof or persuasion concerning the mere rights and sufferings of other living beings will alter the majority's behaviour a jot. Schooled early enough in insensitivity, there are all too many of our kind who can spend a lifetime without experiencing a twinge of pity, although afforded every opportunity to open their minds and hearts to the facts of mankind's pitiless treatment of its own and other species.

This is why it has seemed best to place most emphasis on two other important aspects of the vegetarian argument in this book, showing why we all stand to benefit from a more humane diet in, first, the short term (through adopting a diet for which we are chemically and physiologically better attuned) and, secondly, the long term (because of the ecological and economic facts of modern life that we can no longer afford to ignore). For most of us these are more powerful arguments than anything so irrelevant to our daily lives as mere unkindness to animals. The poverty of the human imagination, the strength of greed, the shortness of memory, the pressures to which we are subjected in business and family life, and our willingness to believe only what we want to believe – these are the barriers that have confronted anyone who has ever taken a clear look at the natural world and has been anguished by the rapacious and pitiless part played by the human race.

Inasmuch as any of us are concerned at all by such matters, most of us are satisfied by what Curtis Freshel called The Legislative Illusion – those measures taken to modify or make acceptable some of our cruelties, rather than to renounce them. It has been said, of course, that if we cared about suffering and injustice; about the facts of politics, poverty and war; about starving nations; about the true extent of child, adult and animal misery that lies below that unsubmerged one millionth of the iceberg that sticks above the sea of newsprint from which most of us make our judgements of the condition of the world we live in – if we really cared about and concentrated on these things 'we should go mad, no doubt, and die that way'. Possibly, in their wisdom, the mind-controllers know, or think they know, that there must be a limit to what we can take.

Yet, even as one writes these words, one knows that the idea is a nonsense. It is just one more thing that it is comfortable to believe. Like the man who sought treatment for his inferiority complex only to be told by the psychiatrist 'But, Mr Jones, you *are* inferior', most of us are quite incapable, in our present state of mis-education and self-obsession, of seeing even ourselves for what we are – far less the world that surrounds us. Most of us can take in little more than our daily problems of personal survival – because that is all we are trained to do. And even these we get wrong, believing (and conveying to our children the belief) that what matters above all is the kind of money we are bringing home, the sort of materially successful image we are showing to our neighbours and the degree of credit our children can bring to us.

These are harsh words. I would be sorry if they antagonized the very people whose imaginations and better feelings I most wish to see expand, but the process of living has taught me that the very most one can hope for is to make a few facts and ideas available to that small but never insignificant minority that is concerned with the fundamentals of human life and values. That minority will have realized that such fundamentals can be imparted only through a more mature concept of education and they will be convinced that, despite apparently over-whelming evidence to the contrary, there can be found within the human heart and mind some spark that, when activated and cherished, will eventually prove that the role of man has not all along been that of the devil's advocate, but rather that of a species destined – self-destined, if you distrust the 'grand-design' concept – to create order out of chaos, reason out of nonsense, purpose out of futile misdirection and the quality of mercy out of a background of almost unrelieved savagery.

What have we made of education to date? We worship academic distinction – mere aptitude for absorbing facts and passing examina-tions. It seems we have yet to learn that it is not the power to absorb facts that makes us properly educated and superior to the other apes, but the power of imagination. The difference between a chimpanzee and an academic can be, in both senses of the phrase, no more than a matter of degree. Only insofar as our imaginations guide and enrich that sponge-like organ we are too often inclined to confuse with a truly developed mind, have we any cause to hope for better things for the world and for ourselves.

If there is any justification whatsoever for our species to be around at all, its function has to be something on the lines indicated in the penultimate paragraph. If we do not believe this to be so, then we must believe in something far worse than any jungle could ever have thought up. We do not need to confuse the issue with religious slogans or sociological jargon in order to see that if mankind continues on its present path of environmental and self destruction it will have achieved far less of real worth than the earthworm or a vulture. If all we can do in the world is to make it bloodier and beastlier and more artificial than it was when our race took the first wrong turning, we would be doing ourselves and our environment a great kindness in bringing the whole episode to a rapid close. A species that has gone so far wrong as has our own is not going to stand still. It must either improve or get worse. I do not believe that the latter choice is necessary any more than it is desirable. I have to believe that the former is possible and if I did not I would not have bothered to write this book.

Authors of other books about the predicament of modern man would probably say much the same. Whether one speaks in dry terms about 'global equilibrium' or, more emotively, about human cruelty and those 'behaviour patterns' that at one time we numbered up to seven and rightly termed 'deadly', the basic concern is, to some extent, shared. We are all deeply disturbed by the way the world is going. It has been my own brief to attempt to concentrate on a single – but I believe immensely important – aspect of mankind's failure to contribute to his environment something he is perfectly capable of contributing if only he can be tempted to see the reasons for so doing.

Cruelty is the worst sin of all. It might almost be called the only one. A form of obsession with self and excluding consideration of others, cruelty has to go before any other reform of ourselves or our environment begins to be possible. The cruelty inherent in our exploitation of the animal world is so undoubted that anyone who has read this far and now finds himself in disagreement with such a statement will have wasted his time, for he will be so far from knowing what I am talking about that he will never have suffered a moment's pang about anything that is going on in the world outside his own immediate circle. I believe and hope that there are few intelligent people who have reached such a low of ignorance and self-obsession, though we have to face the fact that many of us have allowed the scum of daily pollution so to cloud our consciences that the truth and importance of what really matters – of what it is really all about – have been lost to sight.

There is, as we all know, no justification for cruelty. The arguments for humane treatment of other creatures cannot be refuted except by a nihilist. Such arguments are answered not by reasons, but by excuses. When such excuses are accompanied by deference to the theory rather than the practice of idealism, the result is that most human of human failings, hypocrisy. Excuses provide the easy way out, the path of least effort and continued self-indulgence. The educated and intelligent person who pays lip-service to morality and has at least intelligently faced the inexcusable nature of flesh-eating, is more difficult to excuse than the unthinking, who have thought about little and see no alternative. Most of us prefer to fall back on the childish defence of 'But I want to' rather than accept the necessity for self-reform. Dispensing our compassion with absurd selectivity – shedding crocodile tears over the bullfight or the mauled bird brought in by the cat, while in the next breath crooning over the tenderized flesh of the castrated steer or the caponized fowl – few of us have progressed further than the picturebook clichés of our childhood. We want the grass to be green, the sky to be blue and no splashes of red except on the poppies and the instantly recognized 'baddies'.

It is possible to understand and to feel some pity for the weakness and gullibility of our species, but when we look at what our failings have made of the world and the hell that we have created for its more defenceless inhabitants, it is surely incumbent on everyone who can see the total picture to put that understanding at the disposal of those weaker creatures who need it most.

Before it is too late we must become aware that this earth we live on is not anthropocentric. Only man is man-centred. Ecologically speaking, we are totally dispensable. The biosphere is in no way dependent on man and would in fact be much better off without him. The environmentalists who have suggested that man is like a fatal disease that the earth has been unfortunate enough to contract are not indulging in absurd exaggeration. We have the power of choice. We can help what we do. Animals cannot. It is up to us to realize the necessity to ourselves and to our environment to become an influence for good rather than for evil – to learn to live symbiotically instead of like parasites and rogue predators who kill without need or even hatred. The fox, some may protest, kills in excess of need, and therefore animals are no better than man, but if man chooses to upset the local ecology by his own predatoriness and then creates an artificial situation in which a quantity of poultry is held captive in a small area, he cannot complain when a fox starts to behave like a man. We cannot justify our own actions by citing those of a fox or any other animal when man behaves far worse by breeding and slaughtering thousands of pheasants, grouse, cattle, sheep, pigs and other victims of his 'sport' and stomach.

In a way this all boils down to the only viable kind of morality being little more than a sense of balance. In an earlier book I suggested that only by a change of values, not a change of political administrators from the same stable as their predecessors, can people learn to behave more like *humane* beings. Unregenerate people can only create an unregenerate organization and an unregenerate society. Only better people can create a better society. They do not even have to create it – it is already there by the very act of self-improvement. By 'better people' I was meaning, above all, more compassionate people: people who have seen the paramount necessity to eradicate their cruelties. For cruelty is humanity's worst form of imbalance.

There is no parallel in nature to mankind's cruelty. It is a unique vice, peculiar to man and the cause of the major ills of our society. Oddly enough, despite the state of the world by which millions are now downright scared, many still breathe brimstone at the very suggestion that people should become better. They get, it seems, an instant vision of mere goody-goodiness, or interfering busy-bodying, and probably a reduction of their sex life. Let them be assured that although all sorts of baddy-baddiness may well get tidied up in the course of our educating ourselves into a more balanced concept of life and our responsibilities, it is above all cruelty in its many forms that is the evil we must concentrate on eradicating. There is no more constant and widespread example of this evil than in our daily treatment of other species.

The eradication of cruelty is an educational problem, little more, but two great hurdles stand in the way. The first of these is man's fierce resistance to change – personal change, that is, of habits and heart. We all know only too well that one of the major irritants within a consumer society is change for the sake of change, but this relates only to such idiocies as planned obsolescence and other shortcuts to high profits and low standards. The kind of change that can come about through increasing knowledge leading to a revision of habits established in times of greater ignorance is a rarer but much more important phenomenon – but it is coming. Awareness of this necessity to examine old patterns was exemplified some years ago by the views of the executive committee of the Club of Rome in their commentary on the findings published in *The Limits to Growth*, a report for the Club of Rome's project on the predicament of mankind. In each of the points made is to be found an unequivocal concern with the basic problem that has to be resolved – man's preparedness to alter his thought patterns and lifestyle:

> . . . new forms of thinking that will lead to a fundamental revision of human behaviour and, by implication, of the entire fabric of present-day society; . . . an overall strategy must be evolved to attack all major problems, including in particular those of man's relationship with his environment; . . . we cannot expect technological solutions alone to get us out of this vicious circle; . . . to define the balances that must

exist within human society, and between human society and its habitat, and to perceive the consequences that may ensue when such balances are disrupted; ... we affirm finally that any deliberate attempt to reach a rational and enduring state of equilibrium by planned measures, rather than by chance or catastrophe, must ultimately be founded on a basic change of values and goals at individual, national and world levels; ... only the conviction that there is no other avenue to survival can liberate the moral, intellectual and creative forces required to initiate this unprecedented human undertaking; ... the last thought we wish to offer is that man must explore himself – his goals and values – as much as the world he seeks to change. The dedication to both tasks must be unending. The crux of the matter is not only whether the human species will survive, but even more whether it can survive without falling into a state of worthless existence.

Excellent though it was to see such phrases peppering a dry, factual report by environmentalists, scientists, educators, humanists, industrialists and civil servants, it has to be pointed out that they said no more than has been said again and again over the centuries. The trouble has been that the urgency – the threats to mankind itself – have not been sufficiently apparent for the vast majority of people, or even a significant minority, to take a blind bit of notice.

It does not follow that man's new awareness of his responsibilities to his environment has yet shown many signs of recognizing his moral obligations towards other sentient life forms, but it has begun to dawn on him that, as a consequence of his more mature concern for the human race and its total environment, a new attitude towards the so-called lesser creatures is inescapable. If this is not the same thing as a conscious compassion or even a guilty conscience, it is at least a step in the right direction.

If willing to start thinking on these lines, one must, to some extent, be influenced by evidence that many of the greatest names of past and present have not merely anticipated the corporate wisdom shown in the Club of Rome's report, but have made clear that the logical extension of that kind of reasoning must result in, or at least demand, a more responsible and humane concern for the animal kingdom. No 'basic change of values and goals at individual, national and world levels' can prevent man 'falling into a state of worthless existence' unless he is prepared to tackle that violence and cruelty into which he has been schooled throughout the sanguinary history of his species.

And 'schooled' is the right word. It is, I believe, a nonsense – a sophisticated distortion whose perpetuation in all too many spheres has created the second great hurdle to a better concept of education – to suggest that man is innately violent and aggressive. Fear and anger will produce 'aggression' in very many species; but 'aggression' is simply not the right word for that channelling of physical energy that is stimulated by dangerous and provoking circumstances that have nothing to do with a cold and calculated determination to harm or plunder. The bulk of men's cruelty is the result of the barbarous goals and values they have been educated to accept as right and normal. To this very day a high proportion of all taught history focuses interminably upon tediously similar and uninstructive examples of warring, rapacious man's planned abominations against his own kind.

The young are seeing this increasingly and, for all that some of them have taken part in often counter-productive demonstrations that have used or provoked degrees of physical violence, they are reacting against those institutions and vested interests which seek to maintain the exploitational *status quo*. Because they have been taught nothing else, they can hardly be blamed for the fact that much of their reaction has so far been little better than the system to which they are opposed, but their responses to the pressures of militarism, industrialization and the whole web of competitive materialism that shrouds the highly developed areas of the world are – unless an expression of mere political brainwashing – a heartening indication that an instinctual reasonableness still exists.

When we discuss unorthodox matters we tend to forget that while dissenters who voice their arguments stick out like sore thumbs, the majority are silent – not because they have thought whether their habits are responsible, wise or necessary, but because they just have not thought. Very few eminent men or women with a balanced and civilized concern, who have considered the question of mankind's responsibility towards other species, have seriously suggested that it is necessary or even defensible to breed, slaughter and consume the animal kingdom.

On the contrary, while most of them may not have felt the need, or found the opportunity, to make any public or published pronouncements on such matters, it is probably true to say that the majority of those who have considered the matter at all have quite categorically come down on the side of the animals. My dictionary of humane thought, *The Extended Circle*, quotes many well- and lesser-known men and women who have written and voiced their concern. This is not to say that all those who have championed the non-human species have necessarily gone so far as to refrain from eating them. 'A meat diet is far from satisfying', said Livingstone, but lacking evidence to the contrary one suspects he went on being unsatisfied, if for no better reason that that he was so inordinately busy exploring the Zambezi and worrying about the sources of the Nile. We all tend to spend a large part of our time 'worrying about the sources of the Nile', so that rich or poor, famous or failure, we unthinkingly slide into many habits that a moment's quiet consideration would show us to be absurd, inconsistent or even downright anti-social and self-destructive.

It is because it is impossible to over-emphasize the importance of the role education plays in the civilizing process that this book contains the comments of a number of distinguished men and women whose words would have been so much more profitably heeded than the blood-spattered pages of those past-distorting history books and translations of the ancient classics that have done so much to cement the impression that the facts of life have been little more than those of destruction and death. It is the realizations of such men and women that must be allowed to inform that 'reschooling' that Duncan Williams argued so forcefully is essential if the techniques of survival – dependent upon so much more than mere technology – are to be properly learned. Our academic centres, at all levels, are in urgent need of a reasoned compassion. As Williams has written (*To Be or Not to Be*, Davis-Poynter, 1974):

> Reason alone can be hard, unimaginative and selfish; unalloyed passion and emotionalism can be sentimental, cloying and egotistical. The fusion of the two was the *beau idéal* of the best minds of the early eighteenth century, with sentimentality (as opposed to sentiment) waiting in the wings, to emerge from 1750 onwards as the dominant mood both in literary and social terms.

Of the numerous writers who have seen the necessity to relate this fusion to the treatment of those many species we are big enough and brainy enough to dominate and outwit, John Galsworthy is one of those least associated with such realizations. Yet he saw very clearly that all sentient life is an inseparable part of an interrelated pattern. His vision was essentially that of the enlightened environmentalist of today:

> You are not living in a private world all of your own. Everything you say and do and think has its effect on everybody around you. For example, if you feel and say loudly enough that it is an infernal shame to keep larks and other wild song-birds in cages, you will infallibly infect a number of other people with that sentiment, and in course of time those people who feel as you do will become so numerous that larks,

thrushes, blackbirds and linnets will no longer be caught and kept in cages. . . . When a thing exists which you really abhor, I wish you would remember a little whether in letting it strictly alone you are minding your own business on principle, or simply because it is comfortable to do so.

Minding your own business because it is more comfortable to do so is repeatedly cited as a besetting sin of modern man; a part of that cowardice that hardens us against personal change. Enormous indignation, often fully justified, is shown by journalists concerned with human poverty, homelessness and neglect; with baby-battering; with sexism and racism; with landscape destruction, urban ugliness, architectural insensitivity and litter-loutishness; with the problems of old age in a world that cares too little; with the problems of youth in a world that cares too much about exploiting and mis-educating the young. On these and many other issues the socially-conscious media man does much to arouse the feelings of his readers. And good luck to him where his concern is genuine and his facts correct. However, although his strictures have embraced a certain amount of disquiet about factory farming, the export and transport of live animals prior to slaughter, and the barbarities of seal hunting and whaling, seldom does the mass-circulation media permit a genuine and full examination of whether the basic uses to which animals are put can be justified. After all, it is because of these everyday uses of animals that innumerable cruelties are inevitable. If you make your reader or viewer feel really uncomfortable, you may lose him. It is far safer to fool oneself and others that with a little bit of tightening up here and a little more supervision there, everything that we wish to do with animals, and damned well intend to go on doing with them, will soon be within 'permissible' limits of suffering.

We no longer have any excuse for such cowardice and hypocrisy. We are fed with too much information to be able to pretend any longer that we do not know what is done to living, feeling creatures in order that we may cling to the interminable meat-and-two-veg routine that with minor variations is still the centrepiece of Western culinary art.

Some may protest: 'Oh, but things have improved so much lately. People are more concerned. Cruelty and suffering have been reduced to a minimum.' Many of them genuinely gulled by The Legislative Illusion, they point to some Bill passed, usually after repeated readings and blockings in Parliament, to ameliorate one aspect of our fundamentally unchanged insensitivity towards the creatures we wish to eat, chase, torture or wear; and because public concern is still so feeble, such Bills are little more than a sop to minority feeling, their implementation being in the hands of breeders, slaughterers, inspectors and government officials who know all too well the shortness of public memory and the power of commercial interests to override almost any measure that is backed not by the pursuit of profit and power, but by mere abstract whimsy about kindness to animals.

These may seem harsh comments, but the facts about what we do to animals are harsh. Whatever affection individuals may feel for domestic pets, collectively human beings do not allow, and in many cases doubtless feel they cannot afford to allow, pity to influence the decisions that they make in their jobs and social lives. Although it is true that people know more today, and certainly have no excuse for not knowing, their concern has made only short inroads on their behaviour. They are still far more concerned with what other people think about them than with doing what the briefest reflection would tell them is more humane.

But even supposing I have got the balance of despair and hope about right, we do not dispose of the problem by saying 'Yes, how true!' and then ignoring the consequences. We have got to take ourselves in hand, and in order to do this we must face the implication of certain facts. If we can accept that one of these is that modern, Western education has gone tragically wrong in its choice of methods and targets, we shall be thinking on the right lines, but I cannot over-emphasize that, until the violence and cruelty that is enshrined in the educative influence of modern society (by which I mean in the junior schools and the home even more than in the later academic environment) is replaced by something more civilized, the fate of all sentient life – our own, not just the so-called 'lesser creatures' – can only be sad and sanguinary. We get out of life only what we put into it, but for all that this often means that the innocent suffer while the guilty get away with murder.

When we look at what the over-inquisitive, monkey mind of the Aberrant Ape has made of the world, leading us into so many unnatural habits and changing so many aspects of the natural world itself into parodies of what should be, it is not difficult to see why religious and philosophical systems have come about. There are times when many of us must wonder if we are not going mad trying to find explanations for why our species behaves so insanely. Things that are obvious to people who keep their eyes and minds open and receptive are, seemingly, not seen or understood at all by those who 'only think they think'. Our attitude to animal life is very much a case in point. Because they exploit and torment 'inferior' beings, many humans have either not thought about it or persuaded themselves that only their own species can experience real feeling or thought.

Although many pay lip-service to a crude yardstick of suffering based arbitrarily on size or 'cuddle-worthiness' (few hesitate to crush an ant, but feel some pity for a sick or wounded elephant; the koala bear attracts more sentiment than the skunk), most of us will fall over backwards to avoid anything that smacks of that dirty word anthropomorphism. 'Oh, yes, there may be some rudimentary feeling of discomfort', say these sages comfortably on hearing the suggestion that a grouse dying of its maggot-infested wounds under a bush or a stuck pig losing its screams in a gargle of blood, might be experiencing an unpleasant departure, 'but there is no thought there; no anticipation.'

It would be fruitless to argue to what extent each species of animal, bird or fish can feel, think, anticipate or suffer mental or physical pain, but it takes an extraordinarily well-developed state of self-deception to ignore the evidence for animals' ability to experience excruciating levels of physical pain and fear, and even to feel sorrow of a kind and to a degree that is pathetically 'human'.

Higher animals most certainly do think, though their thoughts may be smaller. We do not need laboratory conditions to tell us this. As anyone who has kept a dog knows full well, they reason – if only for short distances. The actions of dogs, cats, horses, monkeys and many other creatures – perhaps, for all we know, even down to the levels of insect life – are quite obviously prompted by reason. Pavlov's experiments told us only what most of us preferred to believe, not what all of us should know.

In some respects animals are streets ahead of us mentally. A dog will telepathically know the thought of a walk in its master's mind even before the coat or boots are put on or a move has been made from the armchair. If, as is well known, animals have this telepathic faculty so much better developed than have human beings, to what extent are our crimes against them even greater than most of us are prepared to admit? If there is doubt in any answer to this question, as there must be, that doubt should alone be enough to make us stay our hands against all other sentient life.

If we think about it – and not many of us do – there are two main nightmares in our world – what men do to each other and what they do to other species. The connection between the two has as yet gone almost unrecognized,[2] yet this is, or should be, what ecological morality is all about. For one does not need to be a seer, a scientist, a sectarian or even a sociologist (who ought to be a compound of all three, but seldom is) to work out the simple but generally ignored fact that the total world situation is not going to be improved if evolution's leading animal imagines that its only moral obligation is towards its own kind. Bible or no bible, cruelty begets cruelty, violence breeds violence, and the exploitation and greed of which man is so uniquely capable cannot simply be switched off like a light when he turns from his rape of the animal world to the difficult problems of social relationships within his own species. As Bruce Allsopp has written, 'Ecological morality requires of the individual that he be the best he can be so that the sum of individual contributions to the communality should be a sum of excellencies' (*Ecological Morality*, Muller, Blond & White, 1972). Allsopp shows a leaning towards the necessity for an eclectic outlook in a world dominated by mind-narrowing specialisms and compartmentalism when he adds: 'We must not seek to achieve perfection along one road, but should, on the contrary, endeavour to create the conditions in which human life may be enriched by innumerable different contributions.'

Human life cannot be enriched in any ultimate or even short-term sense if it pays no regard to our obligations to the rest of 'creation'. It just is not enough to take the easy-going, so-called liberal view of the homely, 'human' kind of man who for reasons that on analysis are probably totally selfish is against the early (i.e., in his lifetime) alteration of the status quo. Our crying need is for the universal and early adoption of at least a basic framework of moral conviction, within which our attitude to animals cannot fail to have a considerable place. Without this framework we are wallowing around in the truly 'permissive' world of non-commitment. 'Oh, tolerance', someone might well have written, 'what crimes have been committed in your name?' Non-violence, or the nearest we can get to it, is one basic the world has got to accept if it is to survive. The necessity to curb our unrestricted human spawning is another. The infestation of a species is in itself a form of violence to the environment. An ecological immorality.

I hope and believe that a few readers at least may have been helped by this book to accept that our species must establish and maintain a beneficial relationship with the rest of nature. It cannot be called beneficial unless it can be seen to extend and evolve permanently into the future. It must be a creative relationship, not a predatory one. Conservation is not enough – least of all that cynical 'concern' that is at root little more than a determination to preserve the environment for humankind's continued exploitation. What this will mean – in our behaviour, in our sense of responsibility towards each other and the rest of the world – must be spelt out for each one of us from the earliest age, and this is what education should be all about.

'Yes, but you have spoiled your case by getting too emotional about it', some may object, as though emotion was one of the major criminal tendencies rather than something of which the world is in great need. In its right place and properly informed it is a vital ingredient. But have I got all that emotional? The bulk of this book deals in hard, often brutal facts, amply supported by science, statistics and common knowledge. Where emotional appeals are based solidly on such facts, no case is thereby spoiled. It merely becomes painfully unacceptable to those who do not wish to accept it. As Brigid Brophy, who writes so brilliantly about our treatment of animals, has said, those who dare to emotionalize about animals are apt to be attacked instantly as sentimentalists, cranks, killjoys, people with no grasp on economic realities, twee anthropomorphizers who attribute human feelings (if not human names and clothes as well) to animals, actually preferring them to humans and readier to succour a stray cat than an orphan child. But such naïveté and shallowness of reaction is surely passing. The wider, holistic picture of which our attitude to the animals is an essential part is being studied with increasing concern. The test of a viewpoint, as Brophy has said, 'is its rationality, not the number of people who endorse it.'

It was Thomas Hardy who wrote: 'The establishment of the common origin of all species logically involves a readjustment of altruistic morals, by enlarging the application of what has been called the Golden Rule from the area of mere mankind to that of the whole animal kingdom.' It may have been Leslie Stephens' essay on Darwinism that prompted Hardy's remark, yet it was only one more restatement of a realization that had been expressed over and over again long before the origin of the species was of interest to anyone. Unless one subscribes to the primitive and shocking belief that animals, being without souls, are fair game for whatever treatment humans wish to inflict on them, the obligation to show pity towards all sentient life is universally recognized as religious in the widest and best sense of that all too often narrow word. There are few religious beliefs that fail to emphasize the need for compassion. Unfortunately there are few scientific specialisms who grant it the least attention. While no theist who conceives of his god as aligned to the smallest degree of mercy can logically dismiss the right of all sentient beings to expect from man more than from the other members of creation evidence of the divine values of pity and love, the scientific mind has as yet shown little sign of awakening to this realization. Yet without it mere knowledge is nothing more than contaminated dust.

Victor Hugo's *grande morale*, clearly sensed by Hardy and the many others whose concerns were religiously based, must be equally valid to the observant scientist and ecologist of the present day; and also to the young, many of whom have benefited from widening communications, have seen more of others' lifestyles, have been appalled by the Establishment's destruction of any but the most mundane idealism and are today searching almost desperately for a philosophy by which to live in a world of increasing superficiality, violence and materialism.

Here, in the wide field of our treatment of other living beings, religion and science are capable of finding a unity on the very highest level of their separate specialisms. Here the balance born of humane eclecticism can bring about a vital and applicable ethic. There is, as was stressed in the first chapter, a moral order within the newly discovered science of ecology. This book has tried to show why a humane diet is, or can be, ecological man's number-one priority. It is becoming daily more obvious that the changeover (we might even say changeback) is to a large extent inevitable, especially if our numbers do not quickly decline. But it is vitally important, if there is a shred of reason for believing that mankind is working out some evolutionary pattern and accepting an obligation or profound need to grow spiritually, that we do the right things for the right reasons rather than for expediency or lack of alternative. I choose to end the main section of this book on a no more flourishing phrase than that, for it is as important as it is sober. I ask you to consider it.

Notes

1. Those content to believe that most animals are humanely slaughtered may care to consider the following facts:
   - electric stunning, a notoriously imperfect practice, is cheaper than the captive bolt, so widely employed
   - stunning is often insufficient to ensure unconsciousness or last long enough. Consciousness is often regained before sticking
   - slaughterers work on a piece-work bonus ('throughput bonus') rather than a quality bonus
   - inspectors may or may not be present, but their main task is in the meat room, not in the slaughter hall

- it is estimated that about one third of poultry go to the knife fully conscious (having missed the stunning tank)
- animals are often stuck without any attempt to stun
- no formal training is given to British slaughterers. Licence is given by local authority on hearsay from the slaughter-house.

Every week in the UK we slaughter some 60,000 cattle, 160,000 sheep, 290,000 pigs, 7-9 million poultry. The sheer quantity of suffering caused can dull the imagination by its very enormity, but it is taking place every moment of every day. (See also Appendix 2.)

2. 'An American study conducted among prisoners in federal jails has shown a close correlation between cruelty to animals in childhood and later aggressive criminal behaviour. Twenty-five per cent of criminals classed as aggressive could remember five or more instances when they had been cruel to animals as against five or six per cent for less violent criminals and 0 per cent for non-prisoners.'

The Veterinary Record, 15 August, 1987

Chapter 9

As old as man

If (man) is not to stifle his human feelings, he must practise kindness towards animals, for he who is cruel to animals becomes hard also in his dealings with men. We can judge the heart of a man by his treatment of animals.

Immanuel Kant, *Lectures on Ethics*

By confining his morality to his own species, man has become the most immoral of all animals; and in so far as the Earth is the Great Mother, and he himself one of her children, man is a matricide. His urgent need, for his own salvation, is a conviction of this sin.

We have failed to understand ourselves and our place in nature because we have been blinded by conceit. Our virtues are real, but they are not exclusive to ourselves. In societies far older than our own, the natural activities of mating, care of the young and group-defence had already led to an expansion of the sense of self to include others, so that the female would give her life for her young and the male would give his life for the group . . . When our dogs show these qualities habitually, we call them instinctive; when we ourselves display them now and then, we call them divine. And this is absolutely typical of the instinctive arrogance of man . . . man is a far more dangerous and unpredictable animal than was the extinct tyrannosaur, and may devastate the Earth by knowledge without love. The study of life without sympathy with it leads at best to a husk of learning and at worst to disastrous results. If we are to be creators and not destroyers, we need knowledge with love, taking from the one a new world-picture and from the other a new ethic.

John Vyvyan, *Sketch for a World Picture*
(A Study of Evolution)

I, for my part, wonder of what sort of feeling, mind or reason that man was possessed who was first to pollute his mouth with gore and allow his lips to touch the flesh of a murdered being; who spread his table with the mangled form of dead bodies and claimed as daily food and dainty dishes what but now were beings endowed with movement, with perception and with voice.

Plutarch

Why should you call me to account for eating decently? If I battened on the scorched corpses of animals, you might well ask me why I did that.
George Bernard Shaw

Nothing more strongly arouses our disgust than cannibalism, yet we make the same impression on Buddhists and vegetarians, for we feed on babies, though not on our own.

Robert Louis Stevenson

We might as well eat the flesh of men as the flesh of other animals.
Diogenes

I have no doubt that it is part of the destiny of the human race . . . to leave off eating animals.

Thoreau

In the eight preceding chapters I have tried to present at least an outline of the case for meat-eating mankind's return to a plant-based diet. The main emphasis has been on the ecological, economic, health and nutritional aspects because these are possibly of most interest to those for whom such ideas are relatively new.

There is, however, a large number of people for whom the history of vegetarianism and the literature of its ethical justification are of equal importance – if for no other reason than that it is comforting to know that so far from being alone in one's concern at the inhumanity of man towards other species, a very large number of past and present men and women have condemned the cruelties we are prepared to inflict in order to gratify our acquired taste for flesh and blood. Among older books little known to the general public must be mentioned Porphyry's *On Abstinence from Animal Food*, Thomas Tryon's *Wisdom's Dictates, Good Housewife Made a Doctor* and *Miscellania*, Humphrey Primatt's *A Dissertation on the Duty of Mercy and Sin of Cruelty to Brute Animals* and Shelley's *An Essay on the Vegetable System of Diet* (possibly inspired by his friendship with John Newton whose work *The Return to Nature*, published in 1811, is thought by some to mark the beginning of the present era of vegetarianism).

Since Shelley's day little of substance was published until Howard Williams' classic work *The Ethics of Diet* and some excellent and equally unobtainable books by the late Henry S. Salt, and the following pages may go a short way to meeting the need for a modern summary of the literature and development of this concern.

The influence of religion

Few thinking people today would deny that the failure of the church to perpetuate a living faith has been due largely to its abandonment of Christianity for Churchianity, and many young people in particular would see the main charge against orthodox religious teaching as being that theology, dogma and ritual have supplanted and obscured the simple moral and spiritual directives of Jesus Christ.

This is very relevant to our theme. The churches' most blatant misrepresentation of Jesus' directives has been in the sphere of violence. As Henry Salt wrote in his powerful book *Seventy Years Among Savages:*

> Religion has never befriended the cause of humaneness. Its monstrous doctrine of eternal punishment and the torture of the damned underlies much of the barbarity with which man has treated man; and the deep division imagined by the Church between the human being, with his immortal soul, and with the soulless 'beasts', has been responsible for an incalculable sum of cruelty.

However, this is not the place to argue the matter in depth; but even the Bible (and one says 'even' for the simple reason that by selecting one's texts from that source one can find approval for practically every good or bad thing under the sun) starts off with God assuring mankind that He has 'given you every herb-bearing seed, which is upon the face of all the earth, and every tree, in which is the fruit of a tree-yielding seed; to you it shall be for meat' (Genesis i, 39). And later, with even more emphasis: 'But flesh with the life thereof, which is the blood thereof, shall ye not eat' (Genesis ix, 4).

If the authenticity of such sources is to be believed, in Edmond Szekely's direct translation of the third century Aramaic manuscript *The Essene Gospel of Peace,* Jesus himself minced no words: 'And the flesh of slain beasts in his body will become his own tomb. For I tell you truly, he who kills, kills himself, and whoso eats the flesh of slain beasts, eats the body of death.'

In his book *The Gospel of the Holy Twelve,* the late G. J. Ouseley offers a translation of the original Gospel which members of the Essene community are said to have preserved from the general corruption. Here is a version of Jesus' teaching that has not been tampered with by the 'correctors' appointed by the ecclesiastical authorities of Nicea. These 'editors', it is said,[1] cut out with minute care the teachings they were disinclined to emphasize or follow, in particular everything that might serve as an argument against flesh-eating, such as the account of Jesus' interference on several occasions to save animals from ill treatment, and even that interesting and important teaching – ever prominent in Eastern scriptures – of the essential unity of all life.

The community in which Joseph and Mary lived did not slaughter a lamb to celebrate the Feast of the Passover. 'Now Joseph and Mary, his parents, went up to Jerusalem every year at the Feast of the Passover, and observed the feast after the manner of their brethren, who abstained from bloodshed and the eating of flesh and from strong drink.'

The Essene text indicates that from childhood Jesus was loving and protective towards animals and birds. 'And to all he spake, saying: "Keep yourselves from blood and things strangled, and from dead bodies of birds and beasts, and from all deeds of cruelty and from all that is gotten of wrong. Think ye that the blood of beasts and of birds will wash away sin?"' The food of John the Baptist was the fruit of the locust tree and wild honey, and the disciples were forbidden to eat flesh food: 'Eat that which is set before you, but of that which is gotten by taking life, touch not, for it is not lawful to you. And into whatsoever city ye enter and they receive you, eat such things as are set before you without taking of life . . . And in the same house remain, eating and drinking such things as they give without shedding of blood . . . Be ye therefore considerate, be tender, be pitiful, be kind; not to your kind alone, but to every creature which is within your care; for ye are to them as gods, to whom they look in their needs.'

It is interesting that the story of the miracle of the loaves and fishes is lacking in this translation. Instead there is a tale of the miracle of the bread and the fruit and a pitcher of water. 'And Jesus set the bread and the fruit before them and also the water. And they did eat and drink and were filled. And they marvelled; for each had enough to spare, and there were four thousand.' And when Judas brings a lamb to be slain for the Passover, Jesus reproves him: 'Not by shedding innocent blood, but by living a righteous life shall ye find the peace of God . . . Blessed are they who keep this law; for God is manifested in all creatures. All creatures live in God, and God is hid in them . . . They in every nation who defile not themselves with cruelty, who do righteousness, love mercy and revere all the works of God, who give succour to all that are weak and oppressed – the same are the Israel of God.'

Jesus was accused of speaking against the law when he quoted Jeremiah's words against blood offerings and sacrifices, and he answered his critics: 'Against Moses indeed I do not speak, nor against the law, which he permitted for the hardness of your hearts', continuing:

> For the fruit of the trees and the seeds and of the herbs alone do I partake, and these are changed by the spirit into my flesh and blood. Of these alone and their like shall ye eat who believe in me and are my disciples; for of these, in the spirit, come life and health and healing unto man . . .

It must be said that Ouseley's sources have not been confirmed by the present writer's research, but if these excerpts are accepted as proof of nothing more, they at least confirm that the Bible was originally a much more comprehensive document than we have today. It would appear that there were no discrepancies between the teachings of Jesus and the philosophy of humane vegetarianism, and it is unreasonable to expect there to be, for Jesus is known to have been a Nazarene – a pre-Christian sect of Syrian Jews similar to the Essenes whose obedience to the Laws of Moses took particular account of the commandment 'Thou shalt not kill.' Their inner orders abstained from both flesh-meats and alcohol. But it is always skating on uncertain ice to resort to lifting passages out of their context. What must influence any responsible student concerned with the specifically Christian attitude to cruelty is not what paragraphs may be quoted from the Bible, nor what the interpretations of church-men may be, but the whole spirit and tenor of Jesus' life so far as we are able to judge it from the texts that have come down to us. Whatever his personal failings and inconsistencies may have been, Jesus Christ was clearly a man who preached non-violence. The extent to which he was able to give attention to the matter of man's violence to other species is not known to us and it may well be that he found quite enough to do in his short life to convince human beings of the basics of better conduct between themselves. Two thousand years later, with the spade work of theory having long been completed, it is easier for us to broaden our concern, which is presumably precisely what Jesus and other great teachers have always expected their 'flocks' to do. Because few of them produced a specific Animals' Charter, we have no right to assume that the lower orders of creation would have been excluded from their compassion. How much more strange had that been the case! 'I say unto you, any cruelty or suffering you may wish to inflict upon animals, this you may do.' It somehow sounds unlikely.

While the Bible may be the most important source of guidance for Western people who feel the need for religious guidelines before being willing to question mankind's cruelty to animals, the main cradle of a more humane concern lay in the Far East. Although in general modern India, Sri Lanka, Burma and Thailand are vegetarian, Tibet and Japan are not – the Zen monks being among the exceptions, and we might have expected them to disseminate a wider interpretation of what must seem to many the unfortunately inconsistent doctrine of *ahimsa* ('non-killing'). The orthodox Hindu is vegetarian, but although Buddhists are forbidden to take life, *ahimsa* being the belief that all life is sacred and that it is man's duty to abstain from harming any living creature, less conscientious Buddhists have for long eaten meat if provided by another. There is even a sutta in the Buddhist scriptures where the Buddha flatly refused to make a strict rule that his monks must be vegetarian on the ground that the *more* strict rule was that they should take and eat whatever was put into their bowls when they went round begging. However, as the eminent Judge Christmas Humphreys, founder and president of The Buddhist Society, has pointed out, since what was given to them would almost certainly be rice and vegetables, the effect on their eating habits cannot have been great.[2]

Furthermore, it should be remembered that Buddhism is second not even to the Holy Bible in the number of interpretations it offers and invites. 'Buddha' is a title (meaning in the Sanskrit 'enlightened', or 'to wake', and equating with Supreme Truth), not the name of a person, and although it is particularly and generally applied to Gautama, the historical founder of Buddhism, it is equally applicable to literally thousands of other teachers, especially in the field of Mahayana Buddhism which subscribes to countless Buddhas and Bodhisattvas (beings who present ideals of life and embodiments of compassion, sometimes loosely called 'Buddhas of Compassion'). Mahayana (meaning 'great vehicle') is the major part of Buddhism and evolved at about the beginning of the Christian era, adding its scriptures to (but not opposing) the Hinayana ('small vehicle') that represented the earliest school of Buddhism (now found only in the Theravada).

Just as 'The Buddha' is equated with Gautama, so is Gautama with the *Dhammapada* (The Path of the Buddha's Dhamma, or Teaching). The Pali version can be read in several English translations, and perhaps this is the best way to judge Gautama's actual attitude to taking life, bearing in mind that the Mahayana scriptures have appeared in Sanskrit, Chinese and other languages for the edification of a world population of Buddhists today estimated to be in the region of 400 million. One sect of the northern (Mahayana) Buddhists were the Shakyas (thought to have lived on the Indian side of the borders of Nepal in the Himalayan foothills) and their scriptural authority was one that left no doubt as to the 'Lord of Compassion's' views on eating meat. The Shakyamuni (Sanskrit, meaning 'the sage of the Shakyas', and a title of Gautama) Buddha says loud and clear:

> To avoid causing terror to living beings, let the Disciple refrain from eating meat . . . the food of the wise is that which is consumed by the Sadhus (Yogis); it does not consist of meat . . . there may be some foolish people in the future who will say that I permitted meat-eating and that I partook of meat myself, but . . . meat-eating I have not permitted to anyone, I do not permit, I will not permit . . . meat-eating in any form, in any manner, and in any place, is unconditionally and once and for all prohibited for all.

And one could hardly say it more flatly than that. However, the incursion of Western values has undoubtedly contributed to some unfortunate broadening of The Middle Path concept, and many Buddhists have extended their eating patterns well beyond the original tenets of their religious belief.

The doctrine of *ahimsa* was developed even more rigorously by the Jains, some one and a half million of whom are to be found in India today. Both monks and the laity are forbidden to eat meat and this concern with the avoidance of taking life extends to hunting and agriculture. A text in many Jain temples reads: 'Non-violence is the highest religion.' Some Jains go so far as to breathe through closely woven cloth in case they swallow an insect and the simple act of walking is seen, logically enough, as of equal danger to the smaller forms of life. Such extremes of concern are admirable, but for most of us, sadly, they are likely to remain only a salutary reminder of the ideal.[3]

The contribution made by the Brahmanas of India should also be noted, and although the monotheistic traditions that developed west of the Indus tended to discourage ideas of compassion towards animals, some Muslim Sufi mystics (who came to be regarded as the Muslims' spiritual leaders) stressed the necessity for a fleshless diet for those hoping to achieve spiritual growth.

But the Bible and the ancient religious systems of the Far East are by no means the only source of early concern for the rights of beasts. Throughout history perhaps no country or religion has failed to develop some degree of ethical or ascetically-based realization of man's relationship to other species. Ancient Greece and Egypt were aware of the religious form of vegetarianism and their myths, like the earliest Hebrew, represented man as having been originally a fruit-eating creature. We now know from our study of physiology and history that these myths were not myths at all, and that men of the stature of Pythagoras, Plato, Diogenes, Ovid, Virgil, Seneca, Porphyry, Plotinus, Plutarch, Horace and Socrates, all of whom advocated a non-flesh diet, were the intuitive and reasonable counterparts of the scientifically knowledgeable modern man who has at last begun to realize that a meat diet is not only unnecessary but, on so many counts, positively inadvisable and unnatural to 'the terminal form of hominoidea' (ourselves). Those who can see only a divide between philosophy and science should notice how often they reach the same conclusions.

Neither the religious nor the secular history of vegetarianism can be covered in a single chapter. To provide anything like a correct and comprehensive account of the humane movement in the Western world alone, one must take into consideration the humanitarianism of Pythagoras, and later of the Platonists and neo-Platonists, which sprang directly from their superior philosophy of harmlessness, mercy and compassion that stemmed through the teachings of Empedocles, Plato and Philo to the Essenes – the sect from which Jesus gained much of his wisdom. Only a revival of this philosophy, opposed and persecuted by the Church and banished by Justinian when he closed the Academy of Athens where it had been preserved, will change the minds and hearts of those who refuse to accept what has not been blessed by the mouthpieces of orthodox Christianity.

The more recent past

The darkest ages eventually detect a dawn. In Europe by the seven-
teenth and eighteenth centuries there was to be seen a renewal of
confidence in the power and potentialities of moral progress. This
humanitarianism (a term which, strictly speaking, denotes devotion to
humanity rather than life in general, but has a wider connotation with
humaneness) brought some revival of sensitivity towards animal suffering. The Pythagorean attitude to flesh-eating was again called to mind
and numerous philosophers and men of letters wrote powerfully against
mankind's callousness to the 'brute creation'.

All through history it has been the proddings and promptings of
concerned writers and speakers that have produced and strengthened
those religions and organizations, sects and groups, that have advocated,
either officially or unofficially, a vegetarian diet. Just as the organizational structure for Western vegetarianism was brought about in the
main by a handful of Bible Christians, so has a minority of articulate
people been essential to such well-known and more obscure orders as
The Adventist Church; The American Natural Hygiene Society; the
Dadupanthi Sadus; the Doukhobors; the Essene faith; the Liberal
Catholic Church; The Order of the Cross; the Carthusian, St Benedict
and Trappist orders of the Roman Catholic Church; the Rosicrucian
Fellowship; The Salvation Army; the Swami Narang and Vishnoi sects;
Taoists; The Theosophical Society; Tolstoyans; the Unity Church; and
the Universal Christian Gnostic Movement. But, as we have seen, the
secular arguments – for all that they may have been prompted by, and
will always be the stronger for, philosophic reasoning and religious
conviction – are in themselves all that is needed for any open-minded
person to judge the strength of the case against cruelty to animals. When
Plutarch wrote:

> The obligations of law and equity reach only to mankind, but kindness
> and beneficence should be extended to the creatures of every species
> and these will flow from the breast of a true man, as streams that issue
> from the living fountain,

and was echoed many centuries later by Addison:

> True benevolence, or compassion, extends itself through the whole of
> existence, and sympathizes with the distress of every creature capable
> of sensation. Little minds may be apt to consider compassion of this
> kind as an instance of weakness; but it is undoubtedly the evidence of a
> noble nature,

they spoke for the thinking and feeling people who have been found in even the most barbarous eras of our history. So many similar sentiments could be quoted, from Hesiod (in the eighth century BC) to the present day, that only the most stubborn or obtuse man could deny that many of the best minds known to civilization have come down uncompromisingly against mankind's long and hideous history of almost unrelieved inhumanity towards the creatures unfortunate enough to share this planet with us.

Leo Tolstoy, who was less than happy that the world wished to honour him for little but his fictional work (which he saw as of infinitely less importance than his religious, social and political writings), was one of the most powerful critics of man's brutality towards other species. In 'The First Step' (*Essays and Letters*) he describes how, when he was walking near Moscow, he saw a pig with its throat already gashed, running away from its slaughterers, only to be caught and finished off. The 'strong, red, coarse carman' who was giving Tolstoy a lift sighed when the pig's squeals had ceased, and asked Tolstoy: 'Do men really have to answer for such things?' Tolstoy comments: 'So strong is man's aversion to all killing. But by example, by encouraging greediness, by the assertion that God has allowed it, and above all, by habit, people entirely lose this natural feeling.'

Much of 'The First Step' is given over to descriptions of slaughterhouses, for Tolstoy was no squeamish theorist. These are no more horrifying than scenes that can be witnessed to this day and every day in abattoirs all over the world, for all that the so-called humane killer and other aids (usually more to do with cleanliness and economics than with humanity) are employed, here and there, to placate the as yet hardly visible stirrings of mankind's conscience. Tolstoy rounds off the essay, which was written as the Preface to a Russian translation of *The Ethics of Diet*, with an unanswerable argument for vegetarianism that includes the following lines:

> . . . if a man's aspirations towards right living are serious . . . he will first abstain from animal food because . . . its use is simply immoral, as it requires the performance of an act which is contrary to moral feeling – killing; and is called forth only by greed and the desire for tasty food.

Tolstoy's objection to cruelty was religiously centred and he rejoiced that the vegetarian movement indicated an evolutionary trend in mankind:

> This movement should bring particular joy to those concerned with
> bringing about the kingdom of God on earth . . . because vegetarian-
> ism is a sign that the aspiration of mankind towards moral perfection is
> serious and sincere.

Tolstoy, of course, was looking at a movement that had not yet been
seriously infiltrated by those whose concern was that a fleshless diet
might bring them better health rather than that it prevented the
breeding and suffering of animals. Before our awareness of the facts of
physiology and nutrition spurred the realization that a natural diet was
obviously healthier than one suiting a different species, nearly all the
great writers and philosophers of the past took a primarily ethical stand
against the exploitation of animals. Plutarch, who has already been
quoted, in his 'Essay on Flesh Eating' laboured both the non-necessity
and the cruelty of the habit:

> Man makes use of flesh not out of want and necessity, seeing that he
> has the liberty to make his choice of herbs and fruits, the plenty of
> which is inexhaustible; but out of luxury, and being cloyed with
> necessaries, he seeks after impure and inconvenient diet, purchased
> by the slaughter of living beasts; by showing himself more cruel than
> the most savage of wild beasts.

'Inconvenient' has become a curiously appropriate term now that the
uneconomic facts of obtaining protein through the bodies of animals
have begun to be brought home to us. It is the continued applicability of
their statements to the modern situation that makes the words of past
writers and philosophers of such particular interest today. Even in
Roman times man's cowardice in aping the majority was held in
contempt by those of freer minds. Seneca wrote:

> If true, the Pythagorean principles as to abstaining from flesh, foster
> innocence; if ill-founded they at least teach us frugality, and what loss
> have you in losing your cruelty? It merely deprives you of the food of
> lions and vultures. We shall recover our sound reason only if we
> separate ourselves from the herd . . . the very fact of the approbation of
> the multitude is a proof of the unsoundness of the opinion or practice;
> let us ask what is best – not what is customary. Let us love temperance
> – let us be just – let us refrain from bloodshed.

It is unfortunate that some men of our times who have *known* better have
not necessarily had the courage to act upon what they knew. Even Albert
Schweitzer, who could write: 'Reverence for life affords my fundamental principle – good consists in maintaining, assisting and

enhancing life, and to destroy, to harm or to hinder life is evil', wobbled a bit at dinner and could temporize with: 'I am conscious that flesh-eating is not in accordance with the finer feelings and I abstain therefrom whenever I can.' However, he was in no doubt that in time all wobblers would accept that:

> Slowly in our European thought comes the notion that ethics has not only to do with mankind but with the animal creation as well. This begins with St Francis of Assisi. The explanation which applies only to man must be given up. Thus we shall arrive at saying that ethics is reverence for *all* life.

And that he was moving towards a more consistent pattern is suggested by his unequivocal statement that:

> The great fault of all ethics hitherto has been that they believed themselves to have to deal only with the relations of man to man. In reality, however, the question is what is his attitude to the world and all life that comes within his reach. A man is ethical only when life, as such, is sacred to him, that of plants and animals as that of his fellow men, and when he devotes himself helpfully to all life that is in need of help.

Einstein, also, agreed with the aim of vegetarianism for aesthetic and moral reasons, affirming that 'it is my view that a vegetarian manner of living by purely physical effect on the human temperament would most beneficially influence the lot of mankind', but like Dean Inge, Byron, von Haller, Paley, Chesterfield and many others he failed to live up to this realization to the same extent as his contemporary, the greatest exponent of non-violence on all levels, Mahatma Gandhi whose statement 'I hold flesh food to be unsuited to our species. We err in copying the lower animal world . . . if we are superior to it' is only to give a passing glance to the views of this remarkable man. 'The basis of my vegetarianism is not physical, but moral . . . I would love to think that all of us who called ourselves vegetarians should have that basis.'

The principle of *ahimsa* was so much a part of Gandhi's outlook, and so taken for granted in India, that little of his thought, except on a political level, has filtered through to the West. A tenuous link between modern East and West is maintained by the American Theosophists' journal, *Theosophy*, but since Sophia Wadia's death *The Aryan Path* has not reappeared, although India's *Theosophical Movement*, the brave little *Sarvodaya, Mira, Gandhi Marg,* and (in England) *The Gandhi Foundation Newsletter* and the Peace Pledge Union's *Studies in Non-Violence* con-

tinue to appear. Men and women of the stature of Sophia Wadia, Vinoba
Bhave, Jayaprakash Narayan, T. L. and J. P. Vaswani, have contributed
significantly both to the emancipation of their country from the threatening bondage of Western materialism and to keeping alive the flow of
humane and humanitarian thought without which the West is in danger
of regarding everywhere east of Suez as territory of interest only to
economists and salesmen. Sadly, however, all too little of the essence of
Eastern belief in man's obligations to the animal kingdom is allowed to
pervade Western thought.

In recent years, numerous British and American writers have expressed with power and feeling their concern with humankind's continued brutality and insensitivity towards its surroundings (see Preface).
There have been some excellent exposures of vivisection, such as John
Vyvyan's *In Pity and in Anger* and *The Dark Face of Science*, Richard D.
Ryder's more recent *Victims of Science*, and Catherine Roberts' *The
Scientific Conscience*. Since Ruth Harrison's classic *Animal Machines*
there have been some books on factory farming and a small handful on
blood sports, but few full-length studies of our largest-scale cruelty to
animals have appeared. Trailblazers included Henry Bailey Stevens'
The Recovery of Culture (Harper & Brothers, 1953), Roy Walker's *The
Golden Feast* (Rockcliff, 1952), and Frank Avray Wilson's *Food for the
Golden Age* (C. W. Daniel, 1954). They have been followed by Stephen
Clark's *The Moral Status of Animals*, Tom Regan's *The Case for Animal
Rights*, Peter Singer's *Animal Liberation* – major contributions from
young academics. Other valuable works include Philip Kapleau's *To
Cherish All Life*, Victoria Moran's *Compassion: The Ultimate Ethic*, J. D.
Whittall's *People and Animals*, Daniel A. Dombrowski's *Vegetarianism:
The Philosophy Behind the Ethical Diet*, Andrew Linzey's *Animal Rights*
(SCM Press, 1976), Keith Akers' *A Vegetarian Sourcebook*, James Ser-
pell's *In the Company of Animals*, Keith Thomas's *Man and the Natural
World*, Rebecca Hall's *Animals Are Equal*, Mary Midgley's *Animals and
Why They Matter*.

At grass-roots level, there has been a welcome increase in children's
books that encourage a more humane interest in animals. This trend is
seen not only in story books, but in more obviously perceptive yet
readable texts for the child reader and for younger children's teachers
and parents. An excellent example is Jane Inglis's *Some People Don't Eat
Meat*. It is far more important to reach young children with humane
ideas than to take on the more daunting task of changing the perspectives of habit-stricken adults!

An almost uncountable number of vegan and vegetarian cookery books are now available and, of those that do more than merely offer recipes, may be mentioned *The New Vegetarian* by Michael Cox and Desda Crockett and *The Vegan Diet* by David Scott and Claire Golding.

Cook books range from the pure and simple (e.g., Kathy Silk's *First Steps in Vegetarian Cookery*, Vegetarian Society, 1979) through the innumerable contributions by Rose Elliot, Colin Spencer, David Scott, Leah Leneman and Sarah Brown, to Alan Wakeman and Gordon Baskerville's *The Vegan Cookbook* (Faber & Faber, 1986) and gourmet recipes that relegate Mrs Beeton to the also-rans.

As Charles Magel's massive *Keyguide to Information Sources in Animal Rights* reveals, the books I have mentioned are only the tip of an iceberg more than 2,000 years old. Strangely, some of the most outspoken critics have had interests and affiliations one might suppose would preclude the championing of 'mere' animals. A number of high-ranking members of the armed services, for instance, have been particularly prominent in their criticisms and even Cardinal Newman – whose Church, sadly, must be numbered among those least concerned with the subservience of the animal kingdom to the whims and greeds of mankind – showed an anger that, although prompted by the barbarities of vivisection, can only logically be applied to all forms of exploitation and cruelty to animals:

> Now what is it that moves our very heart, and sickens us so much at the cruelty shown to poor brutes? I suppose this; first, that they have done us no harm; next, that they have no power whatever to resistance; it is the cowardice and tyranny of which they are the victims which make their sufferings so especially touching; . . . there is something so very dreadful, so Satanic in tormenting those who have never harmed us, and who cannot defend themselves, who are utterly in our power.

I am tempted to end this section with a list of living and very recent writers, philosophers, theologians, scientists, teachers and others who have advocated and to varying degrees followed a meat-free diet. From the recent past people of the stature of William Booth, Krishnamurti, Annie Besant, Isaac Pitman, H. G. Wells, Upton Sinclair and Todd Ferrier spring to mind, but the list of both recent and modern names would be endless and, inevitably, invidious. In any case, no one who needs a who's who of humane concern is a very hopeful candidate for change; he might do better to consider the environmental and economic arguments. But for those who wish to dig further into the historical background to, and the literature of, vegetarianism and humane thought, the following roll of past names (which excludes most of those mentioned elsewhere in this book) offers a useful nucleus:

Apollonius; Akbar; Asoka; Athanasius; Akhnaton; Jacques Bossuet; George Cheyne; John Chrysostom; Clement of Alexandria; Antonio Cocchi; Luigi Cornaro; Charles Darwin; George Daumer; St David; Rukmini Devi; Ralph Waldo Emerson; Epicurus; John Evelyn; Benjamin Franklin; Pierre Gassendi; Jean Antoine Gleizès; David Hartley; Christian Wilhelm Hufeland; Anna Kingsford; Alphonse Lamartine; William Lambe; Justus von Liebig; Carl Linné (Linnaeus); Mahavira; Bernard de Mandeville; Jules Michelet; John Milton; Montaigne; General C. Montgomery; Thomas More; Isaac Newton; John Frank Newton; John Oswald; Origen; Richard Phillips; Alexander Pope; John Ray; Joseph Ritson; J. J. Rousseau; William Shakespeare; Gustav von Struve; Emanuel Swedenborg; Rabindranath Tagore; Tertullian; James Thomson; Hermes Trismegistus; Leonardo da Vinci; Francois Voltaire; Richard Wagner; John Wesley; Zoroaster.

Statements by many of the above can be seen among the hundreds quoted in *The Extended Circle.*

In summary

This has had to be a short chapter, but it may have given some idea of the considerable historical, literary and organizational ramifications of what (for lack of a better single word) is called vegetarianism.

Sadly, few but those already half way towards a more humane attitude of mind can be bothered to seek the opinions that have been expressed on the least admirable aspects of mankind's history. The most popular writers are those who bolster up our weaknesses, gloss over or openly justify and even glamorize our cruelties and offer the same recipe as before. Even those usually more sensitive and civilized writers such as the poets and philosophers tend to be remembered mainly for their least demanding exhortations. How many people know, for instance, that Shelley wrote a powerful treatise on the vegetable system of diet in which he put forward scientific and humane arguments that can hardly be improved upon today? But as Howard Williams wrote in 1883:

That a principle of profound significance for the welfare of our own species in particular, and for the peaceful harmony of the world in general – a true spiritualism, of which some of the most admirable of the poets of the pre-Christian ages proved themselves not unconscious – has been, for the most part, altogether overlooked or ignored by modern aspirants to poetic fame, is matter for our gravest lament. Thomson, Pope, Shelley, Lamartine – to whom Milton, perhaps, may be added – these form a small band who almost alone represent, and have developed the earlier inspiration of, a Hesiod, Ovid or Virgil, the prophet-poets who, faithful to their proper calling, have sought to unbarbarize and elevate human life by arousing, in various degrees, feeling of horror and aversion from the prevailing materialism of living.

Yet today there is a detectable and significant reaction against that materialism. The mounting interest in natural foods and particularly the vegetarian and vegan diets is world-wide and especially noticeable among the young who are the sternest critics of our materialism. It may well be they, and the environmental and economic factors that cannot be ignored in our over-populated, violent and crisis-ridden world, who are combining to transmute the history of vegetarianism into a humane, healthy, inexpensive and practical way of life.

Notes

1. 'After the Council of Nicaea, AD325, the manuscripts of the New Testament were considerably tampered with.'

   Archdeacon Wilberforce (1841-1916)

   'Certain scholars, called correctors, were appointed by the ecclesiastical authorities, and actually commissioned to correct the text of Scripture in the interest of what was considered Orthodoxy.'

   Professor Eberhard Nestlé, *Introduction to the Textual Criticism of the Greek New Testament*

   Edmond Szekely said that the words of Jesus became half forgotten and were not collected until some generations after they were spoken. This can hardly be disputed. Szekely's claim that they were misunderstood, wrongly annotated and many times re-written and transformed, so that the whole truth about the life and work of the Messiah should be falsified and adulterated to make them more palatable, would not seem out of character with the manipulators of ecclesiastical history. Nor can there be any reason to doubt the further claim that the Vatican holds unpublished records concerning Jesus that they feel would endanger the institution of Christian theology.

2. Another non-story, which appears in the Pali Canon and is often quoted by Western people anxious to prove that Eastern nations are no less insensitive

to animals' suffering than they are themselves, is that Buddha died after eating tainted pork. However, as scholars have pointed out, the term 'tainted pork' has an obvious symbolic meaning, concerning the much older tradition that the Buddha gave out too much and brought about the tremendous reaction of the Brahmins against his rashness. Delving into such legends achieves little, especially when language, metaphor and parable do so much to confuse the issue (the word 'pork', for instance, can mean 'esoteric teaching'!), and once again one must take into account the whole spirit and tone of a prophet's life and teachings rather than pick on his isolated remarks, or on those of his alleged spokesmen. As Christmas Humphreys has remarked, 'one cannot imagine the world's greatest teacher eating meat, or for that matter, not knowing that what he ate was tainted.'

3. Of the many factors that are responsible for the continuation of the caste system in India, one is the differences in diet. Acharya Vinobaji has said (*Sarvodaya*, October 1973): 'Out of the 25 million people in Gujarat, 20 millions do not eat meat. The businessmen of Rajasthan and all the Jains of India abstain from it. The Shaivas, Vaishnavas and Brahmins of Maharashtra, Karnatak, Andrha, Tamilnadu and Kerala do not take meat. Thus at least 50 millions out of India's 550 millions never taste meat. Among the rest who do, about 250 millions take it once a week or on festival occasions. Very few have it as a regular meal every day.' He suggests that only a wide acceptance of vegetarianism can bring about a reduction in casteism.

Postscript

In revising the text for this edition I have not updated sources for many statistical and other technical data unless more recent figures show a substantially altered picture. The case for a more humane diet has, if anything, been strengthened since *Food for a Future* was first published in 1975. As long-cherished notions of the essential and desirable nature of a meat-based economy weaken and dissolve in the face of our species' mounting problems of material survival, it is unlikely that the principal reasons for adopting a more responsible diet will merit serious qualification in the foreseeable future.

As this book may have made clear – and as I have no scruple about repeating – I believe that the foundation for rejection of a dietary pattern based on the exploitation of other sentient life is that we learn to be humane for non-expedient reasons if we are ever to realize our human potential. For our own sake, as well as for the animals', we must cultivate the holistic vision.

This and many other books now available give ample facts to back such a viewpoint. In the UK alone some 10 million carcasses are produced for our consumption every week and some 100,000 people are employed in the meat industry. What a 'karma' to have around our necks!

As for obligation towards our own species, consider it in the light of a hard-headed economist's findings. Years ago, Barbara Ward, in *The Economist* of 2 November, 1974, showed why we could no longer justify squandering seven tons of cereal to produce one ton of beef:

> North America's annual consumption per head increased [in the 1960s] from about 1,000 lb to nearly 1,900 lb of cereals – and all but 150 lb of it, through the conversion of animal feeding stuffs, in meat and poultry. Western Europe and the Soviet Union followed on behind. By 1972, at least a third of the world's increased demand for

food reflected increases not in population but in affluent diets.

By the time mechanization, fertilizer, pesticides, transport, processing and super-marketing are added in, at least five units of energy (kilocalories) have been invested to produce one unit of energy in the consumer's actual diet. Changing patterns of demand to higher protein diets have also encouraged the more intensive use of energy. Processing cereals through farm animals not only uses more cereals, it lengthens and increases energy-intensive patterns of production.

The Soviet Union is as committed as any other bourgeois society to the maintenance of meat-eating, if necessary by massive purchase of animal feeding stuffs abroad.

Since 1965, Americans have added 350 lb per head to their annual diet, largely in the form of beef and poultry. This is very nearly the equivalent of an Indian's diet for a whole year. Europeans and Russians are not far behind the Americans.

Again, going back some years, in *Can Britain Feed Itself?* Dr Kenneth Mellanby pointed out that nearly 90 per cent of Britain's 46,919,000 acres of agricultural land goes to support the huge livestock population of 195.5 million – 14.5 million cattle, 28 million sheep, 9 million pigs, 144 million poultry.

Not only do they use the grazing land of 29 million acres, but three quarters of the acreage of tillage is sown with crops for livestock. In addition, many tons of animal feed are imported, much of it from countries where human malnutrition and starvation are rife. When we consume a large steak, we are eating something that may have used enough grain to keep a family in drought-stricken areas of Africa for a week.

We have all the facts. We have had most of them for many years. We know that our distant ancestors were essentially vegetarian, indeed vegan. Even Desmond Morris, in *The Naked Ape* (Jonathan Cape, 1967), wrote:

We were driven to become flesh-eaters only by environmental circumstances, and now that we have the environment under control, with elaborately cultivated crops at our disposal, we might be expected to return to our ancient primate feeding patterns.'

In this edition, on pages 38-39, will be found T. H. Huxley's table of comparative anatomy, confirming humankind's physiological similarity to our fellow frugivore, the anthropoid ape.

We know, too, that not only do most Westerners today eat far more meat than so-called primitive man, but that the quality is so different as to be almost another substance. Our ancestors hunted wild animals that had lived on pasture uncontaminated by men. No one had bred those animals to be fat or to grow quickly. It has been estimated that today we eat seven times as much fat, portion for portion, as those from whom we have descended (an apt word). Those who believe that today's fashion for leaner meat is a safeguard against the health dangers in animal fat are grossly deceiving themselves. Nor can comfort be drawn from our ancestors' lifestyles. It has been suggested that primitive man's meat had five times more polyunsaturated fat in it than today's meat, which is high in saturated fat, much lower in polyunsaturated.

However we look at the matter, whether from consideration of the rights and welfare of other creatures, or the health and survival of our own species, the case for a change of both habit and 'heart' is indisputable. If this book has left you unconvinced, the fault lies in my power of communication, not in the facts.

APPENDIX 1

The formal framework

The eighteenth century brought a new feeling for the styles and values of the classical world. Though much of this interest was centred on the more visible aspects such as architecture and the arts, the literature of the period could hardly fail to acknowledge the humanizing influence in the cultures of Greece and Italy. It was not, however, until the nineteenth century that a more humane way of thinking gave birth to an identifiable philosophy and structure.

By 1842 the word 'vegetarian' came into use, and in 1847 the first secular organization to promote a fleshless diet was formed. It was called The Vegetarian Society and was founded in Manchester, England, owing its existence in large measure to members of the Bible Christian Church founded in Salford in 1809 by a young Anglican clergyman with the somewhat inappropriate name of William Cowherd. Cowherd believed that total abstinence from flesh foods was necessary for spiritual growth, and his congregation pledged themselves to be vegetarian. So convinced were the Bible Christians of their mission that forty-one of them, under the leadership of the Reverend William Metcalfe, emigrated to America, and established a similar Church in Philadelphia. Their numbers steadily increased and their philosophy was strengthened by the support of such men as Dr Reuben D. Mussey (fourth president of the American Medical Association) and the Reverend Sylvester Graham whose research in grains led to the use of the flour of that name for baking. J. H. Kellog, MD, was another strict vegetarian and supported the American vegetarian movement with much enthusiasm.

In 1889 the Vegetarian Federal Union was established, to bring together vegetarian societies from all parts of the world. The first World Vegetarian Congress in Chicago, in 1893 (see *The Incredible World's Parliament of Religions* by Clay Lancaster, Centaur Press, 1987), was followed by another in London, England, in 1897. As a consequence of discussion between societies and individuals, the International Vegetarian Union succeeded the Vegetarian Federal Union in 1908, when a congress was held in Nice. Since then a series of World Congresses has been held in Europe, India, Israel and the USA.

In Europe, Australasia, the Americas, South Africa and various parts of Asia there is mounting interest in a more civilized and healthy pattern of eating. In India, seen by many as the natural home of vegetarianism, despite governmental encouragement of meat-eating, vegetarianism remains strong. Great Britain, with the longest established vegetarian society, has seen a massive upsurge in vegetarianism and veganism in recent years. This has contributed to considerable growth in societies concerned with animal rights and welfare. Continental Europe is also experiencing growth, with societies flourishing in many countries. In Eastern Europe there are particularly strong vegetarian groups in Poland and Yugoslavia.

In the USA and Canada, due to massive problems of distance, the many vegetarian societies tend to be small, but they are now combining their efforts through the North American Regional Organization of the International Vegetarian Union. Animal rights as well as health-orientated groups add weight to the increasingly strong move towards vegetarianism in North America.

Active vegetarian societies are to be found in Washington, DC, Baltimore, San Francisco, Toronto and other main centres of North America, but their proselytizing zeal often falls short of that of the various animal rights groups for whom outreach and conversion are priorities. There are signs, too, that veganism rather than vegetarianism is being seen as the only logical way ahead by the more radical organizations, and this trend is also apparent in the UK.

The *Vegetarian Times* is the USA's national vegetarian publication and has won increasing interest and support in recent years. It can be found in many health food stores, whereas the journals of most of the North American vegetarian societies are limited to their members.

The American Vegan Society's excellent if under-financed publication *Ahimsa* has been run from Malaga for many years by the dedicated Jay and Freya Dinshah. It deserves a much wider readership. Sympathetic to veganism is *The Animals' Agenda* of Westport, politically astute, making good connections with other issues of oppression and concerned with the broader spectrum of animal rights. Although its focus is anti-vivisection, the newsletter put out by PETA (People for the

Ethical Treatment of Animals) of Washington has boosted veganism and deserves to become a standard outreach and educational tool for vegetarian and animal rights groups in the USA.

Of other North American organizations whose concern extends to food animals, the International Society for Animal Rights of Clark's Summit has earned special mention for its uncompromising yet widely respected stance on all forms of exploitation. The Humane Society of the United States has had a less absolutist record, but (by the definition of Harvard University's Office of Government and Community Affairs) is the largest humane society in the USA and has lately shown a more holistic face. Its scientific director, Dr Michael W. Fox, in 1985 widened his activities to initiate the International Network for Religion and Animals to 'bring religious principles to bear upon humanity's attitude towards the treatment of our animal kin.' Its International Advisory Board suggests eclectic intentions.

In the last edition of this book I mentioned The Millenium Guild, founded by George Bernard Shaw's friend M. R. L. Freshel, which gave awards to the authors of outstanding books of humanitarian thought. Currently the Guild seems to be in abeyance, but can be remembered for putting out some fine educational materials in its heyday.

In Britain, the Vegetarian Society (UK)'s journal is *The Vegetarian*, published from the Society's headquarters in Altrincham, Cheshire. It began life in the middle of the 19th century as *The Vegetarian Messenger*, not becoming *The Vegetarian* until 1953. However, The London Vegetarian Society had for some years been publishing concurrently *The Vegetarian News*, and in 1959 the two societies got together to produce a single magazine, *The British Vegetarian*. This turned into a tabloid in 1971 and went through more name and format changes before reverting to its present title.

Complicating matters further, in 1947 Geoffrey L. Rudd, before he became Secretary of *The Vegetarian Society*, launched an independent magazine which he called *The Vegetarian*. In the autumn of 1950 this became *The Vegetarian World Forum*, and in spring 1951 this was shortened to *World Forum*. This was retained until its demise at the end of 1974. Rudd's editing of the magazine ended in 1961, when he handed over to Esmé Wynne-Tyson. Two years before her death she passed it on to James Douglas Macnab in the autumn of 1970. He died four years later, and *World Forum* died with him.

The Vegan began in 1944 as a duplicated news-sheet called *The Vegan*

News. In 1946 it became *The Vegan* and changed to A5 format, which it retained until 1985. For 25 years, until his death in 1983, Jack Sanderson directed the magazine, being joined by Kathleen Jannaway as co-editor in 1973. In 1984 the Society came under new management, and in 1985 the office was moved to Oxford. Colin Howlett took over the editorship from Kathleen Jannaway and the format was changed to A4. Kathleen Jannaway now co-ordinates The Movement for Compassionate Living, the Vegan Way, and edits its journal *New Leaves*.

Despite considerable membership expansion in the 1970s, The Vegan Society is as yet little known outside its membership, but if it can survive the teething problems of its move to Oxford, its logical and needed 'message' can only gather momentum and adherents.

Both *The Vegan* and *The Vegetarian* have been criticized for being too consumer-orientated and non-inspirational, though it cannot be said that their American counterparts have shown a much better track record in this respect, but possibly they should take note of the criticism. In a consumer society, product-boosting magazines easily proliferate. Since the expiry of *World Forum* there has been need of a 'New Age' magazine with a core of those inspirational, philosophical and literary ingredients without which the vegetarian ethic could easily degenerate into little more than dietary choice based on human health and the limitations on world resources. While not neglecting food reform, *World Forum* was not another 'health magazine'. It offered a balance, focussing on the ethical and spiritual and stressing that unity of life without which health in its widest sense is impossible. Its pages are a unique source for research into the history of humane thought.

Other UK organizations concerned with diet-related abuse of animals include Compassion in World Farming whose newsletter *Agscene* is an excellent source of sound information; The International Jewish Vegetarian Society who regularly publish an invaluable journal; The Farm and Food Society; and the undauntable Chickens' Lib whose quizzical name may belie its tremendous work and achievements on behalf of the vast numbers of poultry sacrificed to the British maw.

Fuller details of the main animal rights and welfare organizations can be found in Maureen Duffy's *Men and Beasts: An Animal Rights Handbook*, and in Rebecca Hall's *Voiceless Victims*, both as valuable to old campaigners as to newcomers.

APPENDIX 2

The facts of slaughter and butchery

The following paper was published by The Vegetarian Society (UK) Ltd. in 1986:

Slaughtermen and butchers bear titles honest to the ugly work they do. Even the Government classifies these as offensive trades. No amount of euphemism can redeem processes that are violent, bloody, degrading and cruel. They affront a nation rueing the unnecessary violence in its affairs.

In July 1984 and July 1985 the Government-appointed Farm Animal Welfare Council (FAWC) issued two major reports on the nation's slaughter-houses (or abattoirs, as the trade likes to call them). They, like similar reviews, past and present, make appalling indictments of 'humane' killing: the 1984 report alone made 117 recommendations.

The Government has so far taken no effective action to render even the small mercies required by the FAWC. Animal welfarists have seen all too many earnest reviews pigeon-holed into oblivion; we want to save the FAWC recommendations from this fate by decent, democratic methods that pay a mite of respect to the 4,000 animals slaughtered every minute of every working day. In his or her lifetime the average Briton devours 7 or 8 cattle, 36 sheep, 750 poultry and a dozen or so rabbits, as well as deer (so much for Bambi!).

The ethic of meat-eating assumes: we have the right to take life; the right to breed animals with no other purpose than to kill them for their flesh; the right to force animals to live in totally artificial environments; the right to inflict fear and suffering on thinking and feeling creatures.

Vicious as this cut-throat industry is, its demise must not be attempted by vicious methods. Animal welfarists are commemorating the FAWC reports by urging the Government to act on the advice of its own Council, and we are calling on 'the average consumer' to practise the quality of mercy while the absues continue by eating less meat of all kinds.

The 'humane killer' does not exist. The euphemism alludes to several devices and contraptions to 'stick and bleed' farmed and other livestock (cattle, sheep, goats, pigs, poultry, rabbits, horses and deer).

The industry adheres to an ancient and discredited belief that a better 'bleed out' is achieved if the animal is kept alive long enough (which may be ten minutes) after its throat is cut; accordingly, its heart is beating and it is breathing during this time. It may also experience spells when its sense of pain is not suppressed.

An attempt is made to stun most animals briefly before they are yanked up on a hoist to have their throats cut. They are either hit on the head with a bolt from a pistol or shocked electrically. No attempt at prior stunning is made in ritual (or 'religious') slaughtering by Jews and Muslims, nor for millions of unwanted day-old male chicks, some of which are decapitated with scissors or shears, the rest being suffocated in gas chambers. Stunning by asphyxiation may also be used on pigs.

The violent death-throes of the larger animals may endanger the slaughtermen, who have recourse to pithing rods shoved into the animals' brains which, after provoking an immediate paroxysm of twitching, prolong the period of stunning. Pithing is notoriously un-hygienic.

Satisfactory stunning is often not achieved with the ramshackle equipment – a shambles is no temple of clinical excellence; or the animals come to before they go 'on the rail' to be 'stuck' (have their throats cut). One in three of the two million broilers killed every day in Britain goes to the automatic knives and dismembering equipment still able to feel pain and terror; many go on still sentient into the scalding tanks – the 'redskins' are removed from the oven-readies despatched for sale to the public.

These boring and degrading jobs, which are paid on a headage basis, do not foster nice practices. Slaughterers permitted to dispense with prior stunning on the line for the ritual killing are impatient with the delays entailed in correct stunning methods, which are therefore skimped or dropped from the normal procedures.

Consumers do not like their meat too bloody; their convenience is therefore served by the agonies of bleeding out. The industry callously disregards the evidence that as much blood can be drained from a recently-dead animal, as can be proven by the butchering of game and of poultry whose necks have been wrung.

A few animals are however now being killed by the 'electric chair method' (electric shocks through the heart and brain), with subsequent bleed-out. It remains to be proven that this electrocution at high voltages consistently achieves outright kills in the conditions of industrial slaughtering. Appalling misadventures could occur.

The bled-out animals are butchered – dismembered, disembowelled, flayed and 'dressed' – to yield carcases and joints in their familiar forms. Offal, skin, blood, gut-fill, ordure, bones and fat comprise the butcher's 'fifth quarter', a source both of profit and pollution. A steer would lose, literally, a bucket of blood – about 3½ gallons – before it died, a cow rather more; as much again would be left as the carcase goes to be butchered. Fetuses slide out of pregnant animals as the butchers' knives deliver them in a crude form of Caesarian birth. Meat from fetuses may be passed off in pet-food or in the shady trade in what butchers call 'slink'.

The FAWC investigators suffered an ordeal in witnessing the horrors of the slaughter-house. They objected especially to the 'religious' (or ritual) methods by which Jews and Muslims prepare kosher and halal meat respectively, and they asked the Government for urgent intervention. So far this request has been ignored.

In the Jewish method particularly the animals' suffering is heightened by the appalling ritual of capsizing it in a 'crush' (or 'casting pen') prior to the ritual of 'the cut' as well as by the inadequacies in ensuring instant loss of consciousness. Actually Jews regard most of the meat killed by their own method as unfit for their own consumption, so it is sold, without indication of its origins, through the normal channels. The consumer who might, like the FAWC, abhor such practices could well be buying from 'reputable' butchers and supermarkets meat so produced.

British slaughter-houses are notorious for practices both filthy and cruel. In a review of methods of inspection, Mr C. R. V. Jones, M.Sc., M.R.C.V.S., of the Royal College of Veterinary Surgeons, in *The Veterinary Annual* (20th issue, 1980), noted that 'a number of tests lack precision and accuracy and tend to give equivocal results in the doubtful cases where a definite result is required.' He accepts that 'the handling of viscera and cutting of lymph nodes contributes to the spread of faecal contamination and to the release and spread of bacteria such as salmonellae.'

His further observations must impart after-tastes and taints to the butchers' 'nice, juicy' steaks. Mr Jones comments: 'Examination of the udder by incision will also cause the spread of infecting microorganisms, unless done under strictly controlled conditions, which would be very difficult to impose at abattoirs. The same comments apply to the examination of feet, and this procedure will also soil the inspectors' hands. Soiling of actual carcases by faecal and other forms of contamination is of great concern to inspectors because it is so common at abattoirs in England and Wales. It is a very difficult problem to control, which suggests that the meat-inspection system may be concentrating on unnecessary procedures and forgetting basic concepts of food hygiene.' Potentially dangerous bacteria may lurk in and on 'apparently normal healthy carcases.'

The Ministry of Agriculture reported on the subject in 1985, noting concern that 'practices in some slaughter-houses are unhygienic and pose more of a risk to public health than any deficiencies in premises and fabric. The problems include slack methods of dressing carcases, careless spraying of carcases with water, infrequent sterilization of knives and washing of hands, and inadequate cleaning of the slaughter-hall and equipment. These problems indicate that some local authorities are unable or unwilling to enforce an adequate level of hygiene when plant management fails to do so.'

The Ministry's report recognizes the increase of food-poisoning due to salmonella and clostridia, which should be reversed, with reduced risks to consumers, by better attention to hygiene in slaughter-houses. The Ministry admits that the USA and Canada have not so far been prepared to accept meat from Great Britain because they are not convinced about the standards of supervision. Japan also refuses to accept meat from Great Britain.

'There is growing consumer concern about residues, particularly of chemical substances used as growth promoters and antibiotics', report the Ministry, pleading that the number of compounds to test for and other complications would render surveillance prohibitively expensive. So the consumers are being committed as guinea-pigs in an ill-controlled experiment, with their health at risk and sacrificed at the altar of 'cheap' meat!

In the results of one recent survey, which the Ministry has so far not published, nearly one in four of pigs' kidneys entering the food-chain contained residues of sulphur drugs above the permitted level. This problem is also worrying consumer organizations in the USA.

Meat has certainly 'got the lot'!

In May 1986 the FAWC published its report on Britain's livestock markets. It upheld the complaints long made by animal welfare organizations and recommended 119 reforms. The Vegetarian Society is redoubling its efforts at market monitoring to secure early implementation by the Government and on the spot of the recommendations. The markets, through which 25 million animals a year pass, are cruel relics due for ousting. At the moment, 85 per cent of pigs, 45 per cent of 'clean' cattle and 30 per cent of sheep are sold direct to slaughterhouses. If these animals can be spared the stresses of marketing, so can the rest.

These extracts from the FAWC reports (based mostly on observations made at pre-arranged visits) on current slaughtering practices in Britain give the lie to complacency over 'humane' killing.

- 'We were aware in the course of our enquiry that the slaughter industry was suffering considerable economic problems. It was also evident that in some quarters commercial considerations were contributing to greater pressures on throughputs which in some cases were inconsistent with acceptable standards of welfare. Such a tendency is to be deplored and we would stress the need to ensure that commercial pressures do not cause welfare needs to be overlooked.'

- 'We have seen no evidence on how the animals are affected by being bled in front of each other and in the circumstances must give the animals the benefit of the doubt. We cannot therefore recommend that the law be changed to permit animals to be stuck in front of other animals. Such a change could, in any case, lead to greater callousness among slaughter-house employees.

  Certain safeguards need to be attached to any change in the law: (i) stunned animals must not be dragged over other animals awaiting stunning, nor should they be left in a position where they can be trampled by other animals; (ii) stunning operators must ensure that one animal is properly stunned before moving on to stun another; (iii) noise needs to be kept to a minimum. Consideration needs to be given to the design and positioning of hoisting equipment; (iv) the flow of animals needs to be maintained by careful design of the killing area which takes account of natural behaviour; the use of electrical goads must be kept to a minimum.'

- 'We appreciate that the job is repetitive, dirty, dusty and noisy and that in such conditions there is bound to be a risk of callous and careless handling. The fact that we were informed during our visits that one of the advantages of religious slaughter of poultry compared to slaughter on a fast-moving shackle line was that birds were handled individually and could therefore be treated more kindly and humanely, was not borne out by what we observed.' (We note estimates by Government-appointed inspectors that attempted stunning by electric shocks on the killing line fails in one in three of the 2 million broiler chickens slaughtered every day in Britain. This means that they are fully conscious when their throats are cut, many by machines that can also be faulty, and that a number are consigned to the scalding tanks still able to feel pain.)

Bibliography

In most cases the date and/or publisher of the last known edition is shown

Akers, Keith, *A Vegetarian Sourcebook*, Putnam, 1983

Altman, Nathaniel, *Eating for Life*, Theosophical Publishing House, 1973

Ammerdown Group, *The Transport and Slaughter of Farm Animals*, 1980

Barkas, Janet, *The Vegetable Passion*, Routledge & Kegan Paul, 1975

Berry, Rynn, *Famous Vegetarians and their Favourite Recipes*, Panjandrum Books, 1988

Brambell Report: *Report of the Technical Committee to Enquire into the Welfare of Animals Kept Under Intensive Livestock Husbandry*, Cmnd. 2836, HMSO, 1965

Brophy, Brigid, 'The Rights of Animals', *The Sunday Times*/Vegetarian Society, 1965

Bryant, John, *Fettered Kingdoms*, Remous, 1983

Clark, Stephen R. L., *The Moral Status of Animals*, Oxford University Press, 1984

— *The Nature of the Beast*, Oxford University Press, 1984

Clements, Kath, *Why Vegan?*, GMP, 1985

Cox, Michael and Crockett, Desda, *The New Vegetarian*, Thorsons, 1986

Cox, Peter, *Why You Don't Need Meat*, Thorsons, 1986

Dombrowski, Daniel A., *Vegetarianism: The Philosophy Behind the Ethical Diet*, Thorsons, 1985

Douglas. J. Sholto, and Hart, A. de J., *Forest Farming*, Watkins, 1976

Duffy, Maureen, *Men and Beasts: An Animal Rights Handbook*, Paladin, 1984

Giehl, Dudley, *Vegetarianism: A Way of Life*, Barnes & Noble, 1981

Godlovitch, S. & R., and Harris, John (eds), *Animals, Men and Morals*, Gollancz, 1971

Gold, Mark, *Living Without Cruelty*, Marshall Pickering, 1988

Hall, Rebecca, *Animals are Equal*, Rider, 1988

— *Voiceless Victims*, Wildwood House, 1984

Harrison, Ruth, *Animal Machines*, Vincent Stuart, 1964

Inglis, Jane, *Some People Don't Eat Meat*, , Oakroyd Press, 1987

Kapleau, Philip, *To Cherish All Life*, Harper & Row, 1982

Lancaster, Clay, *The Incredible World's Parliament of Religions*, Centaur Press, 1987

Lewis, John, and Towers, Bernard, *Naked Ape or Homo Sapiens?* Garnstone Press, 1972

Linzey, Andrew, *Christianity and the Rights of Animals*, SPCK, 1987

Linzey, Andrew and Regan, Tom (eds.), *Compassion for Animals: Prayers and Readings*, SPCK, 1988

— *The Song of Creation: Poetry in Celebration of Animals*, Marshall Pickering, 1988

— *Animals and Christianity: A Book of Readings*, SPCK/Crossroads, 1988

Lucas, Jack W., *Vegetarian Nutrition*, Vegetarian Society, 1979

Magel, Charles R., *Keyguide to Information Sources in Animal Rights*, Mansell Publishing, 1988

McCance, R. A., and Widdowson, E. M., *The Composition of Foods*, HMSO, 1973

Mason, Jim, and Singer, Peter, *Animal Factories*, Crown, 1980

Midgley, Mary, *Beast and Man*, Harvester Press, 1979

— *Animals and Why They Matter*, Penguin, 1983

Montagu, M. F. Ashley, *The Nature of Human Aggression*, Oxford University Press, 1976

Moran, Victoria, *Compassion: The Ultimate Ethic*, Thorsons, 1985

Niven, Charles D., *History of the Humane Movement*, Johnson, 1967

Paterson, David, and Ryder, Richard D. (eds.), *Animals' Rights: a Symposium*, Centaur Press, 1979

Porphyry, *On Abstinence from Animal Food*, Centaur Press, 1965

Regan, Tom, *Matters of Life and Death*, Random House, 1979

— *All That Dwell Therein*, University of California Press, 1982

— (ed.) *Animal Sacrifices: Religious Perspectives on the Use of Animals in Science*, Temple University Press, 1986

— *The Case for Animal Rights*, Routledge & Kegan Paul, 1984

— *The Struggle for Animal Rights*, International Society for Animal Rights, 1987
— (with Peter Singer, eds) *Animal Rights and Human Obligations*, Prentice Hall, 1976
Ritvo, Harriet, *The Animal Estate: the English and Other Creatures in the Victorian Age*, Harvard University Press, 1987
Robbins, John, *Diet for a New America*, Stillpoint, 1987
Roberts, Catherine, *The Scientific Conscience*, Centaur Press, 1974
— *Science, Animals and Evolution*, Greenwood Press, 1980
Rosen, Steven, *Food for the Spirit: Vegetarianism and the World Religions*, Bala Books, 1987
RSPCA, *The Slaughter of Food Animals*, RSPCA, 1985
Ruesch, Hans, *Slaughter of the Innocent*, Civitas, 1985
Ryder, Richard D., *Victims of Science*, NAVS/Centaur Press, 1983
Salt, Henry, *Animals' Rights*, Centaur Press and International Society for Animal Rights, 1980
Scott, David, and Golding, Claire, *The Vegan Diet*, Thorsons, 1985
Serpell, James, *In the Company of Animals*, Blackwell, 1986
Sharpe, Dr Robert, *The Cruel Deception*, Thorsons, 1988
Singer, Peter, *Animal Liberation*, Thorsons, 1983
— *In Defence of Animals* (ed.), Blackwell, 1985
Spencer, Colin, *The New Vegetarian*, Elm Tree Books, 1986
Thomas, Keith, *Man and the Natural World*, Penguin, 1984
Turner, E. S., *All Heaven in a Rage*, Michael Joseph, 1964
Turner, James, *Reckoning with the Beast*, John Hopkins University Press, 1980
Vyvyan, John, *In Pity and in Anger*, Michael Joseph, 1969
— *The Dark Face of Science*, Michael Joseph, 1971
Whittall, J. D., *People and Animals*, National Anti-Vivisection Society, 1981
Wilson, Frank, *Food Fit for Humans*, Daniel, 1975
Wynne-Tyson, Esmé, *The Philosophy of Compassion*, Centaur Press, 1970
Wynne-Tyson, Jon, *The Civilized Alternative*, Centaur Press, 1972
— *The Extended Circle: A Dictionary of Humane Thought*, Centaur Press, 1986/Paragon House, New York, 1988

I have removed from this bibliography several more recent works which are of only marginal relevance, though valuable to the holistic debate, and may or may not be out of print. They include Gerald Carson's, *Men*,

Beasts and God (Scribner's, 1972), Doris Grant's, *Your Daily Food* (Faber, 1975), John Nance's *The Gentle Tasaday* (Gollancz, 1975), Ivan Illich's *Medical Nemesis* (Calder & Boyars, 1975), Schopenhauer's *On the Basis of Morality* (Bobbs Merrill, 1965) and E. F. Schumacher's *A Guide for the Perplexed* (Cape, 1977), a book little concerned directly with animals' rights, but of quite as much importance as his better-known *Small is Beautiful*.

Books dealing in the narrower sense with plant foods have had to be excluded, including cookery books, as have most of those in the more technical reaches of health, nutrition, anthropology and other scientific concerns (see, too, chapter 9).

Among other sources of literature and direct action for the advancement of humane thought must be mentioned the vegan and vegetarian societies of the UK, USA, Australia, New Zealand, South Africa and the continent of Europe; the International Society for Animal Rights, Clark's Summit, Pennsylvania, USA; The International Network for Religion and Animals, Washington, DC; Animals Rights Network Inc., Westport, CT; People for the Ethical Treatment of Animals, Washington, DC; Animal Liberation (Australia); Animal Aid; the British League for Animal Rights; The Athene Trust, formed to further the educational work of Compassion in World Farming; the Animal Protection Link; and a large number of anti-hunting, anti-vivisection and humane research societies. Books by Maureen Duffy, Rebecca Hall and Caroline Clough give details of many of these.

Index